Emotional Pedagogy

To feel in order to learn

Incorporating

emotional intelligence

in your teaching strategies

Daniel Chabot

Michel Chabot

Note for Librarians: a cataloguing record for this book that includes Dewey Decimal
Classification and US Library of Congress numbers is available from the Library and
Archives of Canada. The complete cataloguing record can be obtained from their online
database at:
www.collectionscanada.ca/amicus/index-e.html
ISBN 1-4120-4219-4
Printed in Victoria, BC, Canada

TRAFFORD

Offices in Canada, USA, Ireland, UK and Spain
This book was published on-demand in cooperation with Trafford Publishing. On-demand
publishing is a unique process and service of making a book available for retail sale to the
public taking advantage of on-demand manufacturing and Internet marketing. On-demand
publishing includes promotions, retail sales, manufacturing, order fulfilment, accounting and
collecting royalties on behalf of the author.
Book sales for North America and international:
Trafford Publishing, 6E–2333 Government St.,
Victoria, BC v8t 4p4 CANADA
phone 250 383 6864 (toll-free 1 888 232 4444)
fax 250 383 6804; email to orders@trafford.com
Book sales in Europe:
Trafford Publishing (uk) Ltd., Enterprise House, Wistaston Road Business Centre,
Wistaston Road, Crewe, Cheshire cw2 7rp UNITED KINGDOM
phone 01270 251 396 (local rate 0845 230 9601)
facsimile 01270 254 983; orders.uk@trafford.com
Order online at:
www.trafford.com/robots/04-2026.html

10 9 8 7 6 5 4 3 2

Contents

Introduction

A ny teacher, educator, trainer, speaker, coach, in short anyone who engages in a process that consists of teaching someone to learn will ultimately ask himself these key questions :

How do we learn?
Why do some people struggle to learn while others learn easily?
How can we maximize the learning process of those who learn?

Without a doubt, the most troubling question at present remains, why are there so many adolescents who drop out of school? In the United States, for instance, about 25 percent of 13 year-old students do not complete their high school education and the differences between states and cities are huge. In public schools in New York and Washington the percentage reaches 45 percent. Overall one out of every four American children will drop out of the school system without having acquired basic knowledge[1]. Here in Quebec, the percentage of students who will never graduate during their lifetime was 17.5 percent in 2000-2001 while the school dropout rate was 11.4 percent among 15-19 year olds, 22.4 percent among 20-24 year olds, and 26.4 percent among 25-29 year olds[2] in 1998.

In psychology, the term 'learning' is defined as "a relatively permanent modification of the behavior or the behavioral potential resulting from the exercise or the experience that was lived[3]". But during the education process, 'learning' refers much more to the acquisition of knowledge in the classrooms, to the acquisition of practical and technical skills, namely those that are linked to our professional life or to the acquisition of our life's habits such as discipline, responsibility, and motivation. In fact, 'learning' is defined during the education process as "the acquisition and integration of new knowledge in order to reuse them functionally[4]".

In all educational environments, the learning process comes mainly from a formal educational approach, so much so that a good learning process is often linked to a good teaching method. In fact, if a deficiency is observed among our students, we automatically question our teaching methods. For the past few decades, tens or hundreds of teaching methods have been invented, experimented with and, unfortunately, very often put on the back burner. Each time a new method was introduced, its proponent believed that they found THE method that would bypass or solve all the learning difficulties encountered by the students. And how many times has this situation repeated itself?

---

1 These data provided by UNESCO. See www.unesco.org
2 Statistical Report from the Education Dept. (2003).
3 Huffman, K., M. Vernoy and J. Vernoy (2000).
4 Tardif, J. (1997).

Efforts, in this sense, are quite prevalent. A teacher who questions his methods and approaches is undoubtedly very sound and sane, to say the least. Nevertheless, it is possible that the questions one is asking, however pertinent, may be incomplete, i.e., that they only cover one aspect of the entire mechanism involved in the learning process. What we realized is that a high percentage of the teaching approaches, and consequently their evaluations, are essentially cognitive. The reason for this is simply because it is said that the learning process is fundamentally cognitive, i.e., that it basically lies on activities involving the treatment of information[5]. Therefore, we can logically conclude that in such instances where a student is struggling to learn the problem must be cognitive in nature.

In this book, we will take a different position or approach. By no means do we mean to imply that the approach that looks to cognitive methodology for learning issues is irrelevant but instead we feel that it is incomplete and unable to address all of the questions related to the learning process and all of the difficulties attached to it. Therefore, we will shift the focus onto a different area of analysis that addresses other parts of the brain, themselves linked to the development of emotional skills.

Several clues, scientific and intuitive, lead us to believe that emotional skills can explain not just a large part of the learning difficulties encountered but also the learning successes as well. Other researchers come to the same conclusion. In fact, in the monograph « Understanding the brain, toward a new learning science » from the Organization of Economic Cooperation and Development (OECD), we can read the following :

> «*In the past, when discussing goals for education, more discussion centered on how to achieve cognitive mastery through reading, writing and mathematical skills. However, scientists are beginning to realize through experiments what educators have seen in schools; emotions are, in part, responsible for the overall cognitive mastery present in children and adults and therefore need to be addressed more fully. Contemporary cognitive neuroscience provides the tools for performing fine-grained componential analyses of the processing that underlies specific tasks. Such analyses have traditionally focused on cognitive aspects of learning. Similar analyses on the emotional or affective areas have been neglected, as they have not yet been recognized for their role in successful cognitive functions. As such, information in this domain is sparse and incomplete. Lack of measurement and theoretical foundation limits progress of the study of emotional regulation in educational practice [6]*».

One of the main objectives of this work is essentially to provide us with primary basic theoretical elements of a new vision on teaching and learning. Another logical objective would be to propose tangible and integrated applications of emotional intelligence in our teaching strategies.

---

5 Tardif, J. (1997).
6 OECD (2002).

Emotional Pedagogy

It is precisely for these reasons, and many more, that we hereby propose a novel way of understanding the learning and teaching processes which we call emotional pedagogy, an emotional process asserting that in order to learn, one must feel.

Part I

Biological basis for emotional intelligence and learning

Chapter 1

Comprehensive Competencies

L et us open this chapter with a little exercise. Take a few minutes and list all of the qualities that you think are necessary to be a good student. Do the same for the qualities required to be a good teacher.

Traditionally, there were two main types of skills that were recognized, cognitive and technical. Cognitive competency is linked to knowledge and is the most sought after in school. This skill is, in fact, the one that you are currently employing while reading these lines. As far as technical competency, it is linked to the "know how" and everything that has to do with the development of technical abilities such as plumbing or electricity, intellectual abilities such as computer programming, accounting, or practicing law. To these two 'classical' types of skills extends relational competency, our ability to interact with others. This skill is very important and always present each time we communicate with others. Finally, and very recently, we have become aware of a fourth type of skill that we call emotional competency, our ability to experience things, feel emotions, and react accordingly.

We all have experienced situations where our emotions can interfere with other mental and emotional processes. For example, sometimes our emotions overshadow our intellectual, procedural, or relational abilities and sometimes they embellish, enlighten, and facilitate them. This is why it is equally important to pay attention to the development of our emotional skills so that we can take advantage of them in our daily activities.

The brain and the learning process

Thanks to the latest scientific research on the brain, we understand that the types of competencies described above are not only a mindset overview but also a true biological reality. In fact, recent studies have enabled us to understand that each skill has its own specific learning method, its own specific memory system, and even its own specific nervous structures.

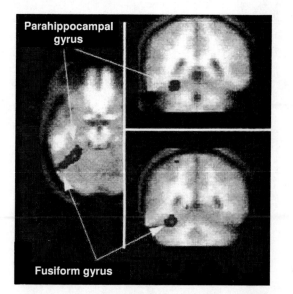

Figure 1.1. Parahippocampal and fusiform gyri, two structures involved in the declarative memory. From Eustachem F. (2000).

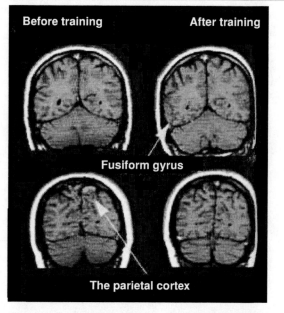

Figure 1.2. During procedural learning, two structures seem to be involved: the parietal cortex (before training) and the fusiform gyrus (after training). From Eustachem F. (2000).

The main nervous structures allowing cognitive learning are the hippocampus and the prefrontal cortex. Therefore, the cognitive competency learning process is made possible thanks to the declarative memory (semantic memory, i.e., knowledge for the meaning of words and how to apply them, and episodic memory, i.e., memory for past and personally experienced events), whose neurological substrates are the hippocampus and the frontal cortex. Works from Dr. Wilder Penfield and neuropsychologist Brenda Milner have clearly demonstrated the very important roles of the hippocampus during cognitive learning[7]. They have shown that when a person has his hippocampus removed, he is no longer capable of acquiring new knowledge.

The technical competency learning process, linked to the "know-how", is associated with the procedural memory, i.e., the memory related to the knowledge of rules of action and procedures and the memory related to the operational knowledge. The countless observations made by researchers on memory have enabled us to understand that the procedural memory works independently from the declarative memory. Brenda Milner and Neil Cohen have noted with astonishment that patients who have undergone a lesion of the hippocampus could learn motor and intellectual tasks even if they had no prior memory of accomplishing these tasks[8]. They could even improve themselves while carrying out these tasks, as a "normal" individual does, with no pre-existing memory of them. Animal research has also confirmed that the procedural memory could work independently from the declarative memory[9]. Therefore, it has been shown that specific nervous structures intervened in this type of memory and learning process (see figure 1.2). This difference between the declarative and procedural memory has been shown for very complex cognitive tasks.

7 See Kolb, B., & Whishaw, I. Q. (1996).
8 See Kolb, B., & Whishaw, I. Q. (1996).
9 Jaffard, R. (2000).

Chapter 1

The relational competency learning process is less known but we can assume that nervous structures and a specific memory are involved. The numerous works on communication, speech, face recognition, and nonverbal decoding have allowed a better understanding of this competency[10].

Finally, the emotional competency learning process relies on an emotional memory that calls the amygdala and the prefrontal cortex into play. The emotional learning process, which will be described in the following chapter, uses a learning method called associative learning. Figure 1.3 shows the amygdala of a human who has undergone aversive conditioning. An unpleasant stimulus (shock on the wrist) has been linked to a blue square on a computer screen. The subjects' electrodermal conductivity allowed the researchers to measure the subjects' emotional reactions during this learning process. In the beginning, the subjects reacted emotionally only following the shock on the wrist. Then, after a few associations between the shock and the blue square on the computer screen, the

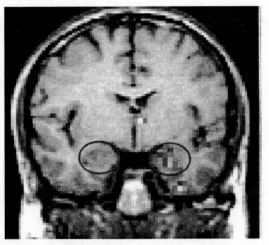

Figure 1.3. The amygdala (circled region), main center of the emotional memory.
From Phelps, E. (2000).

subjects began to show signs of an electrodermal reaction as soon as the blue square appeared on the screen. This reaction is linked to the activation of the amygdala. Several experiments on animals have shown that lesions of the amygdala were linked to a lack of learning conditioned by fear[11].

Neuropsychologist Antonio Damasio has made observations on humans and basically came to similar conclusions as those observed on animals. Subjects with lesions of the amygdala showed their inability to emotionally react to situations involving aversive conditions. Consequently, the inability to learn the relationship between our actions and their emotional consequences can have very important repercussions in our lives. Allow me to share another story[12] with you, the story of Elliot.

Elliot was a very good husband and father and had a very good job with a company that specialized in commercial business[13]. Considered by many as socially, professionally, and personally successful, Elliot was highly regarded by his friends and his coworkers alike. Every task that he undertook was completed with success until the day when he began to have serious headaches. He decided to see a doctor. Following a thorough examination, the doctor discovered that Elliot had a brain tumor. Neurologists agreed that surgery was the only option and opted for the removal of this tumor mass whose exact location was

10 See Kolb, B., & Whishaw, I. Q. (1996).
11 According to Phelps, E. (2000
12 Damasio, A. (1994).
13 This case study from Damasio, A. (1994).

predetermined. But since any operation of this type involved risks, the patient's cognitive and intellectual faculties were assessed beforehand. Hence, the tests given to him confirmed what everyone had noticed : Elliot's intelligence was above average with an IQ of 130.

The surgery, excision of the tumor responsible for his painful headaches, went very well. With several days to recover after the operation, doctors and neurologists had noticed that Elliot was still very sharp and that his intellectual and motor abilities remained intact. But, according to his friends and family members, his personality changed.

After he was released from the hospital, he went back to work where it was determined that he had a difficult time managing his schedule. When the time came to follow a certain set of procedures, he was no longer reliable. As far as reading and filing documents from any given client, however, he was perfectly capable of understanding what he was doing and filing the documents appropriately. He progressed from filing to reading one of the documents with more coherence and intelligence and spent an entire day doing so. However, the quality and progress of his work had been greatly affected. He had become unable to see the global perspective of his work and spent too much time and energy doing things of lesser importance. The admonishments of his coworkers and supervisors did not have an effect on him. Therefore, it was quickly decided that he was no longer reliable. As expected, Elliot was dismissed from his work. He then decided to work in financial investments where he very soon became involved in a suspicious business opportunity despite multiple warnings from his close friends who saw that what he was doing was unethical. As a result of this failed venture, he squandered his life savings and was forced to file for bankruptcy. His wife, children and friends could not understand why a man with such experience and knowledge could be so unreasonable and act so carelessly. His behavior led to a first and second divorce (from a very suspicious wife). Ultimately, he was alone and unemployed.

Astonished, neurologists thought that their patient experienced a sudden decline in his intellectual faculties as seen in other cases. So Elliot underwent new tests and, once again, the results were normal. Neurologists no longer knew how to deal with this case. All they knew was that Elliot's neuropsychological and psychometric tests were remarkable with results that were above average. Even the personality tests were excellent and revealed nothing unusual. But in "real life", he became totally deficient and was not able to either make good decisions or manage his life properly. The specialists felt helpless until one finally recognized their oversight. Elliot was able to recount all the tragedies in his life with an emotional detachment that was not in keeping with the seriousness of what had happened to him. In short, despite the fact that he was devastated financially, emotionally, and personally, and that he went from one failure to the next, he did not seem affected by it. He was able to accurately articulate the sad nature of his situation without expressing the slightest emotional reaction. Neurologists discovered that the surgery he had undergone affected the portion of the brain associated with emotions. Indeed, when images of scenes that normally trigger strong emotions were shown to him (children who suffer from starvation, wounded people, buildings on fire, et cetera) he demonstrated no emotion. He could identify and describe the scenes but did not display any emotions in the process. Yet he was acutely aware that he no longer reacted emotionally as before, that everything left him apathetic; a child's smile, his favorite music, problems in the world, and his deteriorating life. Summarily, Elliot was still able to acquire knowledge but he was no longer able to feel. He was left with the "knowledge" of social, moral and ethical behaviors but was unable to apply it in order to make decisions to manage his life.

What can we conclude from this story? We feel that this story is very informative. For a long time it was believed that in order to make good decisions and manage our lives well, we had to be logical, rational and intelligent (in the traditional sense). In Elliot's case, we have a man who is totally and exclusively logical, rational and intelligent and who can correctly solve any problem that is assigned to him with an inexorable and relentless logic and reason. But in "real life" it is insufficient. Deprived of his ability to become emotional and to feel emotion, Elliot was totally handicapped. He was aware of the disastrous nature of his decisions but could not feel it, hence, could not learn from his mistakes. So we conclude that understanding notions with logic and reason will not always make a difference. In other words, understanding something by using "our head" does not necessarily translate to changes in behavior.

Independent and interdependent competencies

The observations made from Elliot's case have allowed for an understanding that the learning process of each of these intellectual, emotional and social skills was simultaneously independent and interdependent. We noted earlier in this chapter, for instance, that people who have lost their ability to use their hippocampus, following a cerebral lesion or a surgery are no longer able to acquire new knowledge and their cognitive competency is completely compromised. However, they can still improve their technical competency and continue to feel emotions when faced with a situation even if they do not have any declarative memory of the given situation. Another case study reported by Antonio Damasio highlights this last assertion[14].

The case is about David, an individual whose lesions of the hippocampus led to a serious learning deficit where he was totally unable to learn any new fact. For instance, he could not learn a new word or concept, a new sound or location and suffered from a declarative amnesia. Consequently, he was unable to recognize a new person and, as a result, was considered of limited functioning. He lived in an environment totally familiar to him even prior to the outbreak of his lesions. His daily activities were limited to the frequent places he would visit and where he would be offered a cigarette or a cup of coffee. But to do so, he had to interact with people. What is interesting is that he could not recognize the people he

---

14 Damasio, A. (1999).

would talk to, remember their faces or names. Yet, he would selectively associate himself with certain people rather than others. Was it possible for David to develop kinships without knowing the individual? Fascinated by this question, Damasio and one of his colleagues carried out a controlled experimental test that they named "the experiment of the good and the bad boy". Over a period of one week, David was to interact with a few people in three different case scenarios : (1) he would interact with someone who was very friendly and nice (the good boy); (2) he would interact with another person who was very unpleasant and cold and who would engage David in very boring situations (the bad boy); and (3) he would interact with someone who was going to be neutral i.e. neither friendly nor unpleasant (the neutral boy). During five days of preparation, the different situations were scheduled to take place in different rooms with different people that were to play the role of a "good boy", a "bad boy", and a "neutral boy".

At the conclusion of the experiment Damasio and his colleague invited David to take part in two distinct tasks. The first one consisted of looking at pictures of the faces of all the people that he encountered during the week and commenting on whether he knew any of them. Obviously, since he was deprived of his declarative memory, he could recall none of the people. The second task consisted of choosing who among the different groups of four pictures he would feel comfortable going to in order to ask for help or who would he consider his friend? Interestingly, results showed that even if he was not able to recognize the faces in the pictures, in 80 percent of the cases he would choose the "good boy" as a friend or as someone he would trust, never choosing the "bad boy". And when he was asked why he would choose these people, he would not be able to answer.

This fascinating data highlights the key distinction that exists between the different competencies outlined above. In particular, it allows us to see that the cognitive, technical, relational and emotional competencies all work independently. But they also allow us to acknowledge an interdependent relationship between them to the extent that we feel comfortable putting forth the following hypothesis : learning is not a matter of cognitive competency but rather a matter of emotional competency. Below is a remarkable example.
Researchers have conceived a virtual sugar factory[15]. Subjects were managing this factory through a computer simulator and their tasks involved making very quick decisions that would spread over 90 steps. The players managed the production of sugar and had to be involved in the hiring process as well. The goal was to reach the optimal production amount i.e. 9000 tons of sugar. As incredible as it may seem, their work showed that the performance of patients suffering from amnesia (of their declarative memory) improved the same way as their normal counterparts. Despite their inability to remember the slightest detail of their own approach, these patients could still learn as if they had no problem. They had no memory of the way they managed their virtual company yet their results reflected as though they did.

---

15 See Squire, L. and Kandel. E. (2001).

Chapter 1

Here is the conclusion of Larry Squire and Eric Kandel[16], arguably the world's two leading memory and learning researchers :

> *By learning the task (production of sugar), the subject develops a cognitive skill that, at least in the beginning, relies on the development of an "emotion" that tries to assess how to achieve the task. The subject does not memorize the facts of the task but rather develops a general sense or an intuition on how to proceed. Hence, this mechanism is non-declarative, i.e., most of what we call "intuition" is likely to be non-declarative.*

This conclusion from Squire and Kandel is at the very heart of what our concept of learning is, i.e., the learning of a cognitive or technical competency depends essentially on an emotion that tries to figure out how to accomplish the task. We must conclude, a fortiori, that practically nothing applied in the most popular teaching methods takes this key learning process into account. Given that no teachers teach the way they learned, we can assume that they instead teach by way of a method that they learned how to apply. We will elaborate on this point in Chapter 5 when we address how to integrate emotional competency in our teaching methods.

To address the 'proper' brain

One of the main goals of our work is to highlight the importance of the 'emotional' brain in the learning process and its achievements as well. One of the most eloquent studies on this subject is the one carried out at Florida University by Thomas Oakland[17]. Oakland tested 1,554 gifted and non-gifted students between the ages of 8 and 17 to determine whether temperament style separated children who excel in school from children with average capabilities. Using the Student Styles Questionnaire, researchers determined students' preferences in four categories; practical-imaginative, thinking-feeling, organized-flexible and extroversion-introversion. The study's most significant finding was that gifted students are more likely to use a feeling style rather than a thinking style. And while the majority of girls in both the gifted and non-gifted groups tended toward a feeling style rather than a thinking style, gifted boys are 28% more likely to prefer a feeling style than non-gifted boys. You may recall in the introduction of this book the dramatic numbers that differentiate boys from girls with regard to their success in school. It would appear that with gifted boys and girls there is no differentiation as both are likely to use the same temperament style of learning.

This data, which is extremely important for our work, demonstrates the extent to which it is important to address the notion of the 'proper' brain if we want to help students.

---

16 Squire, L. and Kandel. E. (2001) p.90.
17 Harmel Kristin (2000).

When students show signs of learning difficulties we almost always instinctively question their cognitive or technical skills and rarely their emotional one especially if, for instance, their difficulties are in the fields of math., science, or French. For example, Elliot's close friends tried to "reason" with him when it came to helping him make a decision or understand the magnitude of his errors in judgment. The problem, however embarrassing, was that he did understand the logic of his mistakes. But it didn't matter because he was simply unable to feel the effects of his decisions and choices. When he was taking part in a game such as roulette, where each move has consequences, his losses were more pronounced as he was taking foolish risks without measuring their consequences. In fact, even though he may have been able to measure them logically, he was unable to do so emotionally, and so nothing could stop him in his misdirected actions.

In our classrooms, we encounter many students who have emotional difficulties that factor into the learning process. Many parents feel helpless because their children are unable to learn at school yet these children demonstrate the ability to learn certain activities on their own such as memorizing the songs of Madonna or Eminem by heart, being able to create a website or to solve a bug in their computer, et cetera. And what is most troubling for these parents is to realize that their children put more efforts in their non-classroom based daily activities than they do at school. Every teacher knows students in their classroom who struggle when it comes to learning but are well versed in other topics. Often, we have been very impressed while listening to students talk about the topics that were just addressed in the classroom but who subsequently failed in their exams or assignments. It became obvious that their difficulties were not cognitive but rather emotional in nature. Hence, the task was for us to target a part of the brain other than the one we became accustomed to dealing with.

Emotional competency is extremely important when it comes to explaining success in every type of intellectual and emotional pursuit. This has been observed time and again among Olympic athletes whose performances were affected by their emotions. Technically and physically they were at their peak but emotionally they struggled. Ultimately, they paid a higher price. The same applies for countless numbers of students who have a negative "emotional memory" linked to everything that is associated with academic learning and subject matter.

If school and our educational environment are there to highly stimulate and appeal to the cognitive competency, it is a totally different story when it comes to the emotional competency. In fact, the general lack of emotional competency reflects a huge deficiency that can affect students at school and in any educational environment. This is why we believe that the introduction of emotional intelligence in teaching and learning strategies is an exceptional avenue that should be explored in the future.

Chapter 1

To appeal to the 'emotional' in our teaching methods

In the future when teaching strategies are addressed, we should make it a priority to understand the importance of emotions and emotional competency as part of the learning process as therein lies the essence of the approach that we call emotional pedagogy. We mentioned earlier that we are all highly familiar with the cognitive approach typically used in education. Indeed, as soon as a student encounters academic difficulties, our first reaction is to question their intellectual abilities or their cognitive strategies especially if we don't call into question our own teaching methods. Here is an example to illustrate this point.

Imagine that you are interested in playing golf and you want to become a good player but you know nothing about this sport. So you decide to go to the library around the corner and buy the best book on golfing that describes the technique, the learning methods, and every trick to become an excellent golfer. Because you are very motivated you read the book with great interest and assimilate its entire content. You become so familiar with the terms described in the book that you soon begin to discuss the sport with long-time golfers. In fact, as they listen to you, these long-time golfers avoid the idea of playing against you because they assume that you are an excellent golfer. They are convinced that one cannot talk about the sport with such knowledge and not know how to play. The question that arises is this, if it is obvious that your knowledge of golf does not guarantee that you are a good player, can the knowledge of golf accelerate the process of learning the technique? When we ask this question to our seminar attendees, the majority reply, yes, i.e., that there is no doubt that the cognitive learning will have a positive effect on the technical learning. By knowing the theory it is possible to avoid making elementary mistakes or simply to adjust the basic technique. Let us ask the question differently. Can my theoretical knowledge of golf slow down the process of learning the technique? Unfortunately, the answer is yes. My cognitive competency can favor technical learning but can also be detrimental to it precisely because of our emotions.

Let us narrow down our observation. Imagine that every time you hit the ball it systematically goes a little to the right and always ends up hitting the trees. Your first reaction will be to try to understand why this is happening and you will tap into your logic and reason to find an answer. But imagine that you find the answer in the book or from a coach who gives it to you. Will this change anything? Not really! Better yet, you could ask yourself, "I understand why the ball always ends up hitting the trees, but it will not change anything because once I hit it I know where it will end up". So if 'knowing' will not make a difference, what will? The answer lies in what any good coach in golf or in any other field will tell you, "stop thinking and start feeling". And we have all experienced this 'concept' at one point or another. What we are trying to say is that the real learning process in any field takes place when we feel rather than when we understand.

Comprehensive competencies

Other research, somewhat disturbing, in the field of education has shown that there was no correlation between academic and professional success. Daniel Goleman observed : "When we traced back the career of 80 Harvard students of the 1940s time when the IQ of students from top east coast universities presented greater differences than today we realized that those who had the best scores in class were not as successful in terms of salary, productivity and professional status as those who did not score well. Moreover, they were neither happier in their private lives nor more satisfied with their existence[18]." Other research has shown that emotional competency was twice as important as cognitive and technical competencies combined when it comes to explaining success in any field[19].

Cognitive versus Emotional brain

As we have seen, competencies are guaranteed by specific structures in the brain. The table below summarizes the main characteristics of each competency.

Table 1.1
Different competencies and their characteristics

Characteristics	Competencies			
	Cognitive	Technical	Relational	Emotional
Main Function	To think	To do	To Communicate	To feel
Functioning Mode	Logical and rational	Motor and intellectual	Verbal and nonverbal	Irrational and impulsive
Learning method	Cognitive	Procedural	Experiential	Associative
Memory	Declarative	Procedural	Relational	Emotional
Structure of the brain involved	Hippocampus and cortex	Cortex, fusiform gyrus, cerebellum	Cortex	Amygdala and prefrontal lobe

Numerous connections have been discovered between the limbic system and the prefrontal cortex. A famous case in neurology was the Phineas Gage story. Phineas Gage is the first patient from whom we learned something about the relationship between personality and the function of the front parts of the brain that had been damaged following an accident. His rational intelligence remained intact but his emotional intelligence was severely damaged as seen in his irrational and impulsive behavior when he was upset.

---

18 Goleman, D. (1995).
19 Strickland, D. (2000).

The Phineas Gage case, which includes many different behaviors, allows us to draw a very distinct table on the functioning modes of the rational and emotional brain. The rational brain, as its name indicates, is rational and logical. It functions in a systematic and orderly fashion. It knows speech and can verbally communicate. Its judgment is based on its perceptions and its logic. The moment new information is received, the rational brain gives it careful consideration and stores it in its conceptual system. Conversely, if new information does not make it to the conceptual system the rational brain can either reject it or question its belief system. Moreover, this rational brain is guided by its beliefs and values. Its learning method, as we've mentioned, is cognitive and its declarative memory involves the hippocampus.

As for the emotional brain, it is completely irrational, impulsive, and reacts spontaneously. As soon as something annoys, threatens, disturbs or irritates it, it will react without analyzing or considering the subtleties of the situation. Since emotional reactions are sometimes intense, the rational brain can easily be dominated by them in a way that can alter our judgment and perceptions as we will show later. The emotional brain is dominated and controlled by its impulses and needs. Its learning method is associative and relies on the emotional memory that involves the amygdala.

In addition, we know that all these competencies influence one another. We all have experienced failing an exam at one time or another simply due to the stress even though we mastered the topic. In this case, the emotions are responsible for disturbing the cognitive competency. We could quote similar examples for technical or relational competency. Conversely, other research has shown that positive emotions could help improve the cognitive and technical learning processes. This has enabled researchers to note that 80 percent of success was due to emotional intelligence against only 20 percent for IQ[20].

In the beginning of this chapter, we invited you to draw a list of qualities of a good student and a good teacher. Table 1.2 shows the four main categories of emotional competency involved in academic learning and success.

Table 1.2
The four categories of emotional competency useful for academic success

Communication	Motivation	Autonomy	Self-management
Clear-minded	Curiosity	Autonomy	Focused
Able to listen	Engagement	Resourceful Discipline	Self confidence
Empathy	Interest	Initiative	Control
Team spirit	Passion	Open-minded	Optimistic
Daring	Perseverance		Patient

20 According to Goleman, D. (1995).

Observation table on your student's emotional competency

In order to determine your student's emotional competency, we propose, as illustrated below, an observation table that you can fill out for each student.

Student name : _____

Group : _____

1 Not At All	2 Very Little	3 Little	4 A Fair Amount	5 Much	6 Very Much

Communication

1.	When he expresses himself, his ideas are clear even if he is under pressure and emotional.	1 2 3 4 5 6
2.	When I talk to him, he listens, and is very present and attentive.	1 2 3 4 5 6
3.	He is sensitive, tolerant and compassionate to others.	1 2 3 4 5 6
4.	When he works in a group, he shows cooperation, contributes to the team effort, and is always there when the group gets together.	1 2 3 4 5 6
5.	He is not afraid to ask questions, suggest answers, and share his opinions.	1 2 3 4 5 6

Motivation

1.	He is inspired by a desire to know and understand new things.	1 2 3 4 5 6
2.	In class, he is not an observer but an active student involved in his learning process.	1 2 3 4 5 6
3.	He has a strong interest in his classes.	1 2 3 4 5 6
4.	He is a passionate student.	1 2 3 4 5 6
5.	He has perseverance even when facing difficulties.	1 2 3 4 5 6

Autonomy

1.	He is autonomous.	1 2 3 4 5 6
2.	He is resourceful.	1 2 3 4 5 6
3.	He has a good working discipline.	1 2 3 4 5 6
4.	He takes a lot of initiatives, in his actions as well as when he brings ideas.	1 2 3 4 5 6
5.	He is very receptive to new ideas and to new ways of doing things.	1 2 3 4 5 6

Self-management

1.	I have a feeling that his personal issues do not interfere with his studies or his contacts with others.	1 2 3 4 5 6
2.	He has self-confidence and trusts his own abilities.	1 2 3 4 5 6
3.	He remains calm when facing most problems.	1 2 3 4 5 6
4.	He is optimistic most of the time.	1 2 3 4 5 6
5.	He is calm and patient.	1 2 3 4 5 6

Chapter 1

Compiling Results

For each question from the table, transfer each score to the figures below. Do this for each of the four categories; communication, motivation, autonomy and self-management. Then connect each value with a line, graphing your student's entire emotional competency.

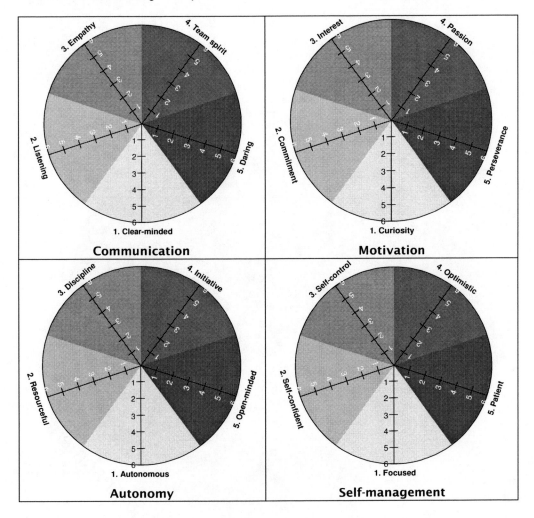

You can now add up each section and transfer the results in the figure below. Then connect each value with a line, creating a graph representing your student's entire emotional competency.

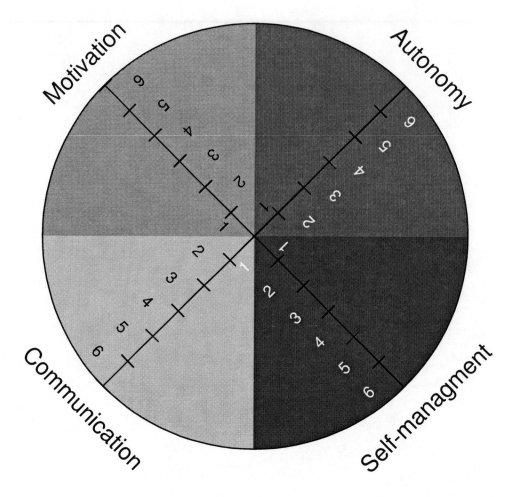

Chapter 1

In the second part of this book, we will concentrate on the way to stimulate the emotional competency of the pupil. But first we must understand that in order to stimulate his emotional competency we must rely on our own experiences with this notion because there are no teaching methods that teach emotional competency. It must begin within us, with our own feelings. In other words, we must use our own emotional intelligence to be able to stimulate our students.

Firstly, we will examine the emotional competency of a good teacher and evaluate those qualities. Table 1.3 shows the four main categories of emotional competency necessary to teach.

Table 1.3
The four main categories of emotional competency necessary to teach

Communication	Motivation	Adaptability	Self-management
Able to read nonverbal	Love for his work	Adaptable	Calm
Charisma	Credible	Accommodating	Focused
Clear-minded	Discipline	Avant-garde	Self-confidence
Able to listen	Available	Creative	Control
Empathy and compassion	Engagement	Diplomat	Optimistic
Enthusiasm	Team spirit	Know how to behave	Patient
Sense of humour	Inspire confidence	Flexibility	Perseverance
Stimulating	Interest	Open-minded	Positive
Sympathetic	Passion	Strategic	Serene

Questionnaire
Self-evaluation of your emotional competency as a teacher

Instructions : For each statement below, circle a number (1 to 6). Do not choose according to what you want or would love to become, but according to what you really are. Be spontaneous and circle the first thing that comes to mind. In some cases, you will have to try to imagine how others perceive you.

1	2	3	4	5	6
Not At All	Very Little	Little	A Fair Amount	Much	Very Much

	Communication	
1.	I perceive the emotional state of my students according to their nonverbal signs such as : body posture, tone of voice, facial expression, skin color, perspiration, or shakiness.	1 2 3 4 5 6
2.	My personality commands respect from my students.	1 2 3 4 5 6
3.	When I speak, my ideas are not confusing even under pressure or when I am emotional.	1 2 3 4 5 6
4.	I can feel my student's emotions and understand them.	1 2 3 4 5 6
5.	I feel like I understand my students very well when they speak to me about a problem.	1 2 3 4 5 6
6.	I radiate a good energy when I teach.	1 2 3 4 5 6
7.	I have a good sense of humour in my class and with my students as well.	1 2 3 4 5 6
8.	I stimulate my students in class	1 2 3 4 5 6
9.	I make it easy for my students to approach me.	1 2 3 4 5 6
	Motivation	
1.	My students notice my love for teaching and for my class subject.	1 2 3 4 5 6
2.	I feel like I am credible in the eyes of my students.	1 2 3 4 5 6
3.	I adopt the same discipline as the one that I expect from my students.	1 2 3 4 5 6
4.	I stop to help a student in need even if my schedule is busy.	1 2 3 4 5 6
5.	I instill, in my students, the commitment to their work, projects, exams, et cetera.	1 2 3 4 5 6
6.	In class, I impart a climate that favors collaboration and teamwork.	1 2 3 4 5 6
7.	My approach arouses a feeling of self-confidence in my students.	1 2 3 4 5 6
8.	In my class, I arouse interest in my students.	1 2 3 4 5 6
9.	I am a passionate person.	1 2 3 4 5 6
	Adaptability	
1.	I can easily adapt to unpredictable situations.	1 2 3 4 5 6
2.	I make things easy for my students to carry out their work, exams or projects.	1 2 3 4 5 6
3.	I like to explore new avenues in my teaching skills.	1 2 3 4 5 6

Chapter 1

4.	I am innovative, inventive and creative in my classroom.	1 2 3 4 5 6
5.	I address my students with tact and diplomacy.	1 2 3 4 5 6
6.	I find it easy to establish relations with my students.	1 2 3 4 5 6
7.	When I teach or approach my students, I consider their specific needs.	1 2 3 4 5 6
8.	I encourage my students to use different ways of learning then my own to help them reach their goals.	1 2 3 4 5 6
9.	I have a strategic pedagogic approach.	1 2 3 4 5 6

Self-management

1.	I remain calm when faced with stressful situations.	1 2 3 4 5 6
2.	My personal issues do not interfere with my teaching and my contacts with students.	1 2 3 4 5 6
3.	I have confidence in my ability to help students who have problems.	1 2 3 4 5 6
4.	I remain calm when faced with the majority of problems.	1 2 3 4 5 6
5.	I am optimistic most of the time.	1 2 3 4 5 6
6.	I am patient with my students.	1 2 3 4 5 6
7.	I have perseverance when it comes to helping students who struggle.	1 2 3 4 5 6
8.	I remain positive even when things do not work the way I want.	1 2 3 4 5 6
9.	I am rarely disturbed by events.	1 2 3 4 5 6

Compiling results

For each question of your evaluation, transfer each score to the figures below. Do this for each of the four categories; communication, motivation, adaptability and self-management. Then connect each value with a line, creating a graph representing your entire emotional competency.

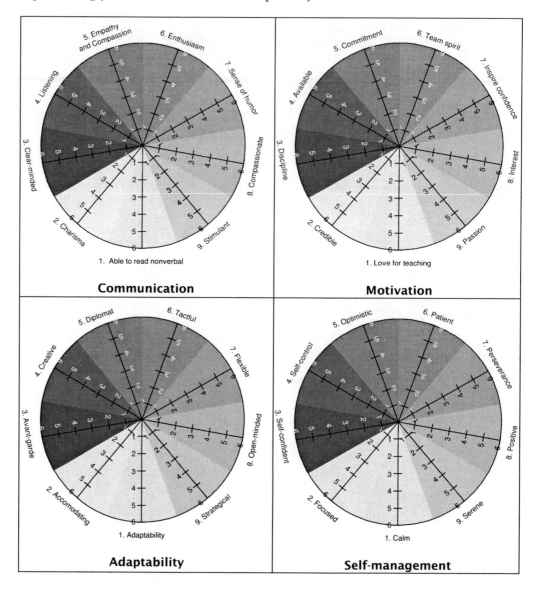

Communication

Motivation

Adaptability

Self-management

You can now add up each section and transfer the results in the figure below. Then connect each value with a line in order to end up with a graph representing your entire emotional competency.

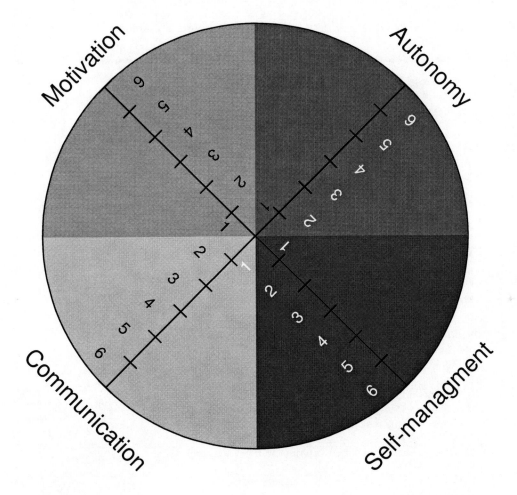

Questionnaire
Evaluating the teacher

Instructions : Read each statement below and keep in mind that they apply to your teacher. For each one, circle the number (1 to 6) that best describes the teacher in terms of his method of teaching and the way he interacts with you and other students.

1	2	3	4	5	6
Not At All	Very Little	Little	A Fair Amount	Much	Very Much

Communication

1.	My teacher perceives my emotional state according to nonverbal signs such as : my body posture, my tone of voice, my facial expression, my skin color, my perspiration, or my shakiness.	1 2 3 4 5 6
2.	My teacher has a personality that commands respect from his students.	1 2 3 4 5 6
3.	When my teacher speaks, his ideas are not confusing even under pressure or when he is emotional.	1 2 3 4 5 6
4.	My teacher can feel my emotions and understand me.	1 2 3 4 5 6
5.	My teacher understands me when I speak to him about a problem.	1 2 3 4 5 6
6.	My teacher radiates a good energy when he teaches.	1 2 3 4 5 6
7.	My teacher has a good sense of humour in his classroom and with his students as well.	1 2 3 4 5 6
8.	My teacher is stimulating.	1 2 3 4 5 6
9.	My teacher makes it easy for his students to approach him.	1 2 3 4 5 6

Motivation

1.	My teacher clearly shows his love for teaching and for his subject matter.	1 2 3 4 5 6
2.	My teacher is credible in the eyes of his students.	1 2 3 4 5 6
3.	My teacher adopts the same discipline as the one that he expects from his students.	1 2 3 4 5 6
4.	I can feel that my teacher is available to help me even if his schedule is busy.	1 2 3 4 5 6
5.	My teacher encourages me to commit to my work, projects, exams, et cetera.	1 2 3 4 5 6
6.	In his class, my teacher imparts a climate that favors collaboration and teamwork.	1 2 3 4 5 6
7.	My teacher knows how to arouse a feeling of self-confidence in me.	1 2 3 4 5 6
8.	In his class, my teacher arouses interest in his students.	1 2 3 4 5 6
9.	My teacher is a passionate person.	1 2 3 4 5 6

Adaptability

1.	My teacher can easily adapt to unpredictable situations.	1 2 3 4 5 6
2.	My teacher makes things easy for me to carry out my work.	1 2 3 4 5 6

	exams or projects.	
3.	My teacher likes to explore new avenues in his teaching skills.	1 2 3 4 5 6
4.	My teacher is innovative, inventive and creative in my classroom.	1 2 3 4 5 6
5.	My teacher addresses me with tact and diplomacy.	1 2 3 4 5 6
6.	My teacher finds it easy to establish relations with me.	1 2 3 4 5 6
7.	When he teaches or approaches me, my teacher considers my specific needs.	1 2 3 4 5 6
8.	My teacher encourages me to use different ways of learning then his own to help me reach my goals.	1 2 3 4 5 6
9.	My teacher has a strategic teaching and learning approach.	1 2 3 4 5 6

Self-management

1.	My teacher remains calm when faced with stressful situations.	1 2 3 4 5 6
2.	I can feel that my teacher's personal issues do not interfere with his teaching and his contacts with students.	1 2 3 4 5 6
3.	My teacher seems to have confidence in his ability to help students who have problems.	1 2 3 4 5 6
4.	My teacher remains calm when faced with the majority of problems.	1 2 3 4 5 6
5.	My teacher is optimistic most of the time.	1 2 3 4 5 6
6.	My teacher is patient with his students.	1 2 3 4 5 6
7.	My teacher has perseverance when it comes to helping students who struggle.	1 2 3 4 5 6
8.	My teacher remains positive even when things do not work the way he wants.	1 2 3 4 5 6
9.	My teacher is rarely disturbed by events.	1 2 3 4 5 6

Comprehensive competencies

Compiling results

After the students have filled out the questionnaire, you can average each question and transfer each score to the figures below. Do this for each of the four categories; communication, motivation, adaptability and self-management. Then connect each value with a line, creating a graph representing your entire emotional competency.

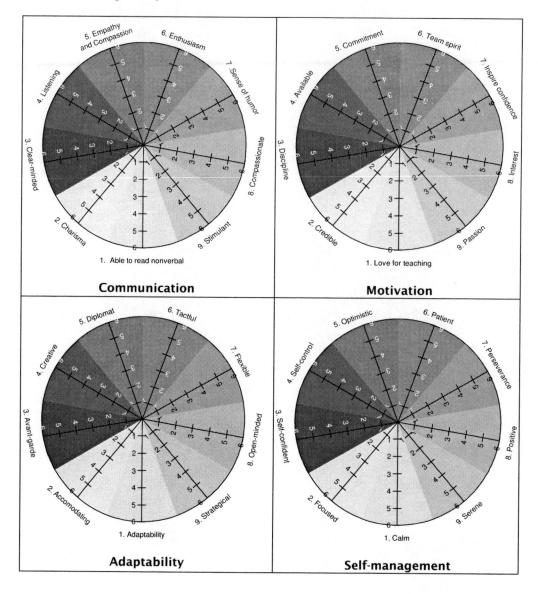

You can now add up each section and transfer the results in the figure below. Then connect each value with a line, creating a graph representing your entire emotional competency.

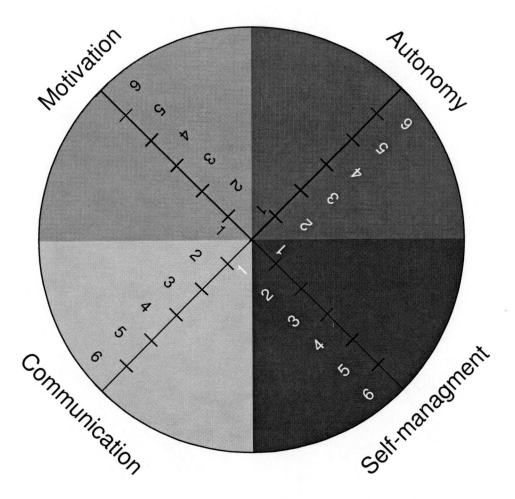

Chapter 2

Emotions and their impact on the learning process and the academic output

I n the previous chapter, we have insisted on the fact that emotional competency was at the heart of the 'learning process' matter. Far from underestimating other competencies, the emotional one is probably the most important for the simple reason that, human beings are essentially emotional. Let us examine in depth what emotions are and what their impact on the learning process is.

The word 'emotion' comes from the verb 'to move' which means "to set in motion". This is perhaps why when we are moved by something we sometimes use the expression "something is happening inside". In the word 'emotion' we also find the word "motion" which has the same root as the word "motor" or "engine". So we can say that our emotions are powerful "engines" that set us in motion in a sensible manner as much internally as externally.

Primary emotions

Many scientists have become interested in different aspects of our emotions. One of them, Paul Ekman[21], has visited different peoples and has identified seven primary emotions; fear, anger, sadness, disgust, ontempt, surprise and joy. Ekman has discovered that each of these emotions has its own characteristics and can be found in the cultures that he visited regardless of race, language, religion or customs.

---

21 Ekman, P (1982).

Researchers have, therefore, been able to establish the link that exists between emotions, their Triggers, and the resulting behaviors. For instance, we know that fear is triggered by a potential threat which results in a flight response whereas anger can be associated with an obstacle that prevents us from reaching our goals and leads to an attack designed to eliminate the source of frustration. As for sadness, it is linked to a loss and triggers a withdrawal. The surprise emotion is activated by an unexpected situation which leads to an orientation response that will put our body in a state of alert so as to be able to evaluate the potential dangers of the situation. The disgust emotion is usually induced by an aversive situation that leads to rejection. An example is when we swallow something poisonous and the substance is expelled from our body. This physiological response can save our lives. Contempt is a special emotion. As explain Paul Ekman[22] «Contempt is only experienced about people or the actions of people, but not about tastes, smells or touches. You might, however, feel contemptuous toward people who eat such disgusting things, for in contempt there is an element of condescension toward the object of contempt. […]We feel superior to another person when we feel contempt, those who occupy a subordinate position may feel contempt to their superiors.» Finally, joy is triggered by the manifestation of a desired situation which leads to an 'approach' behavior. From a purely biological standpoint we can easily understand why our primary emotions are important and play a role in our individual and collective survival.

Table 2.1
Triggers, emotions and behaviors

Triggers	Emotions	Behaviors
Threat	Fear	Flight
Obstacle	Anger	Attack

---

[22] Ekman, P. (2003).

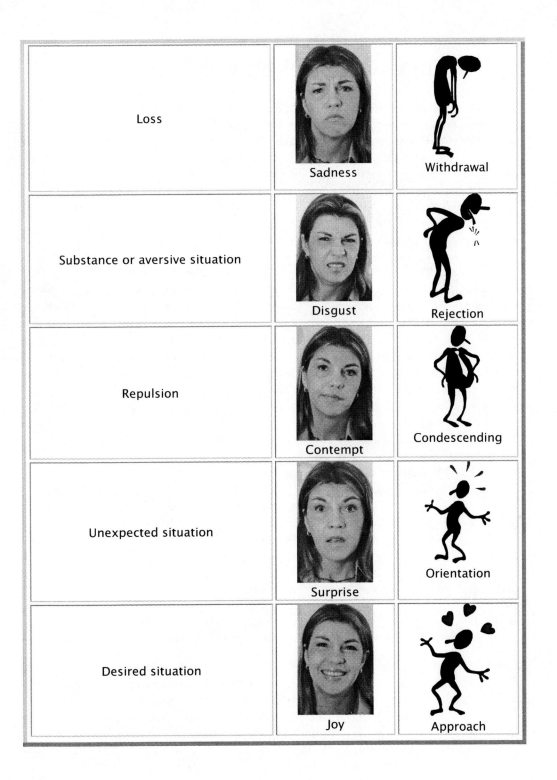

Loss	Sadness	Withdrawal
Substance or aversive situation	Disgust	Rejection
Repulsion	Contempt	Condescending
Unexpected situation	Surprise	Orientation
Desired situation	Joy	Approach

Secondary and social emotions

The six primary emotions described by Ekman help ensure our survival. However, we can often feel these emotions even if our survival is not at stake. In fact, primary emotions are the raw materials from which all other emotions can be built. And it is through our learning process that we can develop emotions linked to the many situations and circumstances of our daily lives. This is when secondary and social emotions come into play (see table 2.2).

Table 2.2
Secondary and social emotions

Fear	Anger	Sadness	Disgust	Mépris	Surprise	Joy
Anguished	Exasperated	Affected	Annoyed	Discredited	Astonished	Cheerful
Concerned	Frustrated	Ashamed	Antipathetic	Haughtiness	Astounded	Comfortable
Frightened	Furious	Contrite	Ashamed	Offended	Impatient	Confident
Guilty	Hateful	Crushed	Aversive	Repelled	Impressed	Content
Horrified	Hostile	Deceived	Bitter	Revolted	Insecure	Delighted
Indecisive	Impatient	Dejected	Disgusted	Sicken	Shaken	Enchanted
Insecure	Imprisoned	Depressed	Embittered	Underestimated	Stupefied	Enthusiastic
Intimidated	Irritable	Disoriented	Humiliated		Troubled	Euphoric
Jealous	Irritated	Distressed	Hurt			Excited
Perplexed	Jealous	Humiliated	Imprisoned			Flattered
Pre-occupied	Mad	Hurt	Intimidated			Happy
Ridiculed	Offended	Jealous	Irritable			In love
Shy	Restless	Melancholic	Jealous			Joyful
Suspicious		Nostalgic	Loathed			Merry
Terrified		Overwhelmed	Offended			Optimistic
Timid		Saddened	Repelled			Passionate
Tormented		Sorry				Relieved
Trapped		Tacit				Satisfied
Uncertain		Vulnerable				Secure
Worried						

Whether we talk about the insecurity of not understanding a topic or the frustration experienced following a failure or the deception of a bad score when we expected a higher one, it is our life experiences that make us feel these emotions. Likewise, when we feel emotions that are more connected to our education and morals such as guilt, shame, jealousy, shyness, or humiliation, it becomes more evident that these very emotions were learned. Feelings of guilt and shame are not innate but rather learned via the relationships that we make between various life situations and their consequences. All secondary and social emotions are learned and are all derived from primary emotions. Therefore, our education and culture play a huge role in the learning of these emotions which,

Chapter 2

like primary emotions, result in a large number of behaviors. Table 2.3 shows examples of secondary and social emotions that are tied to the learning process.

Table 2.3
Secondary and social emotions at school

Triggers	Emotions	Behaviors
Discomfort in the school system (threat)	Insecurity (fear)	Dropping out (flight)
Difficulties with certain subjects (obstacle)	Frustration (anger)	Criticizing the system (attack)
Failure (loss)	Deception (sadness)	Demotivated (withdrawal)
Reprimand and contempt (aversive situation)	Humiliation (disgust)	Detachment (rejection)
The teacher give a negative feedback to a student (Repulsion)	Contempt	The student reply disrespectfuly to his teacher (Condescending)
Unexpected results (unexpected)	Amazement (surprised)	Irritation (orientation)
Success and encouragements (desired situation)	Enthusiasm (joy)	Motivation, interest (approach)

If we take a closer look at these emotions, it is clear that out of all six basic emotions only one is truly positive. This is why it becomes crucial to develop our emotional intelligence so as to maximize all the emotions that are derived from joy. This will help generate behaviors geared toward approach and motivation and ultimately benefit schools and classrooms as well. These emotions are omnipresent and can interfere throughout the learning process by altering it. But before we elaborate on this point, we would like you to do this exercise below.

Emotions and their impact

Exercise 2.1
Identify the Trigger, the emotion, and the behavior

From the stories described below, try to identify the Trigger(s), the emotion(s), and the behavior(s).

Karen's story[23]
Karen is incapable of asking her teacher questions when she does not understand his explanations. He often encourages students to ask questions but Karen is unable to do so. She refrains from asking questions and often remains uncertain when it comes to doing her homework.

Briefly summarize the facts :

Emotion(s) felt by Karen :

Trigger(s) :

Behavior(s) :

Tom's story[24]
Tom is not comfortable with the idea of working on a project with other classmates. Since it is mandatory, Tom decides to do it. At the first group meeting, he is rather cold and does not express himself much. At the end of this meeting everyone is given a task to complete. When the meeting is over, Tom meets his friends and complains about his teammates saying that it is always the same and he is always left with the most difficult task.

---

23 Corrected version of Karen's story :
    Fact : The teacher encourages students to ask questions
    Emotions : Shy – Timid
    Behaviors : Avoids asking questions
    Triggers : Being judged by her peers or her teacher represents a danger and a threat
24 Corrected version of Tom's story :
    Fact : Work in a team project
    Emotions : Worried – Shy – Insecure – Frustrated - Annoyed
    Behaviors : Hesitant to carry out a projet – Cold and speaks little – Complains about his colleagues
    Triggers : Fear (worried, shy, insecure) : The possibility of working more than others represents a threat
    Anger (frustrated and annoyed) : Obstacle in the sharing of tasks
    Disgust (annoyance) : Aversive situation from the fact that he would prefer that things be different

Chapter 2

Briefly summarize the facts :

_____

_____

_____

Emotion(s) felt by Tom :

_____

Trigger(s) :

_____

_____

Behavior(s) :

_____

_____

_____

Peter's story[25]

Peter just received the result of his semester's project. The score was below his expectation. In fact, when he saw it he was shocked, started to curse and criticize the teacher, and expressed how the project was unfeasible and that the teacher was too harsh with the way he scored the project. He then crumpled his work, nearly destroying it. When he got home, he did not greet his parents and quickly went to his room to study.

Briefly summarize the facts :

_____

_____

_____

Emotion(s) felt by Peter :

_____

Trigger(s) :

_____

_____

_____

Behavior(s) :

_____

_____

_____

---

25 Corrected version of Peter's story :
        Fact : Receiving a bad score in his project
        Emotions : Surprised – Frustrated – Annoyed – Disgusted – Disappointed – Affected
        Behaviors : Shocked - Cursed - Criticized the teacher - Crumples his work – Does not greet his parents – Quickly goes to his room
        Triggers :   Surprise : unexpected score
                        Anger (frustration, annoyance) : obstacle in the passing of his class
                        Disgust (annoyed, disgusted) : the bad score represents an aversive situation

Emotions and their impact

Jennifer's story [26]

Jennifer is leading a workshop on communication. Someone's cellular phone is ringing a first time. Jennifer then reminds the participants about turning their cellular phones off. A few minutes later, the same cellular phone rings again. Jennifer raises her voice and warns him to turn it off. As the ringing persists, Jennifer demands that the person goes outside the room to answer his call.

Briefly summarize the facts :

Emotion(s) felt by Jennifer :

Trigger(s) :

Behavior(s) :

Now describe a situation that you have experienced and try to analyze it in minute details.

Briefly summarize the facts :

Emotion(s) felt :

---

26 Corrected version of Jennifer's story :
    Facts : While Rose is leading a workshop, a cellular phone keeps on ringing
    Emotions : Irritated – frustrated – furious
    Behaviors : Asks participants to turn off their cellular phones – Raises her voice –
    Demands that the participant leaves the room
    Triggers : The ongoing phone rings and the participant's attitude represent an obstacle
    for Rose in her workshop

Trigger(s) :

Behavior(s) :

How emotions are learned

The learning of emotions is associative meaning that it is very much like the Pavlovian type. Let us remember that in the beginning of the century famous Russian physiologist Ivan Pavlov was conducting research on the digestive system. His work with dogs revealed that the production of saliva was involved in the digestion process. Pavlov discovered that when food was presented to dogs they would salivate excessively. But one day, to his greatest astonishment, he found that the salivation in dogs was not linked to the food but to the sound of the saucepans used to carry food. Intrigued by this observation, Pavlov decided to expound on the experiment.

His approach involved inserting a tube in the dog's mouth to collect the saliva and then measure the amount. He used the sound of a bell as a neutral stimulus and meat as an unconditional stimulus.

The experiment was carried out in three steps :

STEP 1.
Before the experiment, the sound of the bell produces an orientation reflex but no salivation. This is why it is called a neutral stimulus.

Still before the experiment, the meat is able to trigger a salivation response. This is why it is called an unconditional stimulus capable of triggering an unconditional response (salivation).

Emotions and their impact

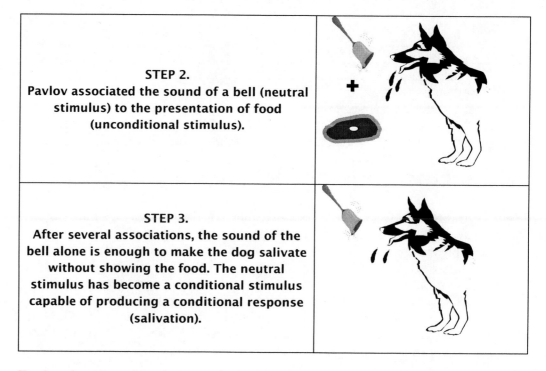

| STEP 2.
Pavlov associated the sound of a bell (neutral stimulus) to the presentation of food (unconditional stimulus). | |
| STEP 3.
After several associations, the sound of the bell alone is enough to make the dog salivate without showing the food. The neutral stimulus has become a conditional stimulus capable of producing a conditional response (salivation). | |

During that time, American psychologist John B. Watson, also had knowledge of Pavlov's work and was very fascinated by it. He maintained that all emotions and behaviors were the result of a conditioned behavior (Pavlovian type). Needless to say, this assertion created much controversy and disagreements. Watson[27], therefore, decided to scientifically demonstrate that our emotional learning was similar to the one demonstrated by the Pavlov test. So he worked with a 9-month old child named Albert who he conditioned following the same steps as Pavlov's :

27 Watson, J. B., et R. Rayner. (1920).

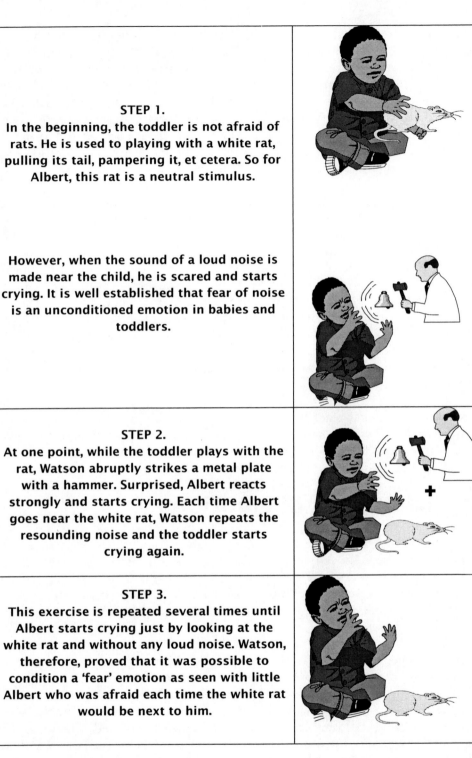

STEP 1.
In the beginning, the toddler is not afraid of rats. He is used to playing with a white rat, pulling its tail, pampering it, et cetera. So for Albert, this rat is a neutral stimulus.

However, when the sound of a loud noise is made near the child, he is scared and starts crying. It is well established that fear of noise is an unconditioned emotion in babies and toddlers.

STEP 2.
At one point, while the toddler plays with the rat, Watson abruptly strikes a metal plate with a hammer. Surprised, Albert reacts strongly and starts crying. Each time Albert goes near the white rat, Watson repeats the resounding noise and the toddler starts crying again.

STEP 3.
This exercise is repeated several times until Albert starts crying just by looking at the white rat and without any loud noise. Watson, therefore, proved that it was possible to condition a 'fear' emotion as seen with little Albert who was afraid each time the white rat would be next to him.

Following Albert's emotional learning, he started to manifest unexpected reactions such as fear of white rabbits, white teddy bears, and Santa Claus' white beard. In short, he was afraid of every object or animal with a white fur. We call this phenomenon : generalization, which leads the subject to react to any

Emotions and their impact

stimulus that presents similar characteristics to the conditioned stimulus. This phenomenon is very important because it allows us to understand the majority of our emotional reactions. And because there is a distinction between emotional memory and declarative memory (memory of the facts), it is possible to have no memory of how and when such a situation has made us react emotionally. Very often we have no memory of the facts that surround a learned emotion while traces of the emotions remain. The emotional memory does not retain precise details but rather the general aspects of a situation. Hence, as soon as a sign arises the emotional reaction is suddenly engaged and the emotion emerges.

We can easily imagine many situations that take place in schools and classrooms. For instance, a student is struggling to understand a certain subject and is humiliated by other students and reprimanded by his teacher. All of these elements merge in his emotional brain and create an emotional memory that can intensify. Thus, any school can become an environment where a vast number of emotional associations can be made between situations, academic subjects, teachers, et cetera, and can be equally as positive as they can be negative. However, emotions do not always lead to the expected behaviors. For example, a teacher who calls a student 'stupid' because he does not understand what is being taught to him can leave traces in his emotional brain leading to aversive and defensive behaviors that could impede his learning process and consequently result in him dropping out.

There is no doubt that teachers are very concerned about doing their jobs well just like parents have always been with their children. But it is possible, even with the best intentions, that some teachers may embrace approaches that could precisely lead to the opposite effect than the one that is sought.

The 'background' emotions

The notion of 'background' emotion is not very popular when we address the concept of emotions. Indeed, when talking about emotions, we generally refer to the primary ones described by Ekman (fear, anger, sadness, disgust, surprise and joy), as well as the secondary and social emotions (embarrassment, shyness, jealousy, shame, guilt and pride). But what about the background emotions that are permanently present?

To use an image, let us think of a movie scene where we have the front layout representing primary and secondary emotions that are explicit and very visible. This layout constitutes the main action plan in other words, the plan that we focus our attention on and that shows the action between actors. So the scene could be a dialog between two actors on a very crowded sidewalk. The background could show people walking by, cars passing by and a lady walking her little dog. And all this background action is bolstering the front layout where our attention is focused on. Yet it becomes important to understand that the background action is equally important. Imagine if the two actors were still and having a dialog in the rain. People in the background would be restless because of the weather and because they are drenched. Thus the "weather" will play a different role by triggering different emotional states in the background people depending on whether it is sunny or rainy. And so background emotions are what we feel when we are "tense" or "relaxed", "gloomy" or "cheerful", "discouraged" or "enthusiastic", and "anxious" or "serene".

The primary emotion arises spontaneously and abruptly with a high peak and a rather sharp decline. The secondary emotion can last longer but the sensations associated can be very pronounced. However, background emotions are erratic and their duration is longer. For instance, let us assume that you receive bad news and become upset. A specific aspect of the news triggers this anger. Once the emotional peak of the anger that you felt has subsided, a feeling of irritability could still remain with you throughout the day; you may still tend to your daily routine but not without this "diffused anger" as a

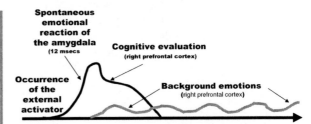
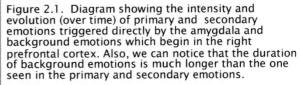

Figure 2.1. Diagram showing the intensity and evolution (over time) of primary and secondary emotions triggered directly by the amygdala and background emotions which begin in the right prefrontal cortex. Also, we can notice that the duration of background emotions is much longer than the one seen in the primary and secondary emotions.

background feeling. Despite this feeling, you will still smile at your students when you say 'hello' but internally you will be annoyed by what happened in the morning, carry this feeling throughout the day and perhaps not sleep well at night. Yet a meticulous observation could highlight specific aspects of your background emotion. For instance, we could see that something is missing in your face when you are smiling or when you are shaking a hand, or even in your tone of voice. In short, background emotions also include expression elements that are nonverbal and more subtle, but as real as the ones found in primary and secondary emotions. Other revealing background emotions are; body posture, the degree of mobility of the head, neck and limbs, erratic, jerky movements, facial vitality, brightness of the eyes, and inflection of the voice, to name a few. Teachers must be able to recognize and identify all of these characteristics in their students for it will help them to be aware of what is happening in their class.

Antonio Damasio[28], the first to define background emotions, differentiates primary from secondary emotions. Table 2.4 reviews these differences.

---

28 Damasio, A. (1994).

Table 2.4
Differences between primary, secondary and background emotions

Primary emotions	Secondary and social emotions	Background emotions
The triggering factors are generally external. For instance, threat, obstacle, or loss can trigger fear, anger, or sadness and are external.	The triggering factors can be external (for instance, seeing a face we are familiar with) or internal (for instance, the memory of a friend and the fact that he just died).	The triggering factors are generally internal. For instance, you more or less consciously mull over your colleague's criticism. The image that you have of the situation is as much in the background as the emotion associated to it.
The trigger is immediate and directly activated in the amygdala.	The trigger is immediate and activated in the amygdala. However, the prefrontal cortex is involved in maintaining the emotion.	The trigger, though relatively quick in certain situations, is progressive and wavy. It involves the right prefrontal cortex and the hippocampus, which sends signals to the amygdala.
They manifest at the musculo-skeletal level : muscular tension in the limbs with increased heart rate required for the fight or flight response.	They manifest at the musculo-skeletal and visceral levels.	They manifest at the visceral level : For instance, the tightening felt in the stomach, the solar plexus and the throat, and the heartache feeling.

If there is no doubt that primary and spontaneous emotions such as fear, anger or sadness interfere with the learning process, it is very likely that the emotions that create the most damage are the background emotions. Let us take a closer look at the impact of emotions on the learning process.

Emotions and their impact on the learning process and the academic output

Where were you and what were you doing on Sept. 11th, 2001 when you learned about the attacks on the World Trade Center? Most people have a very detailed memory of this historic moment. Personally, I was in my car and on my way to College to give a class. I heard the news on the radio. The memory I have of this event is still very fresh and will probably remain in my mind for the rest of my life. Likewise, the day John Fitzgerald Kennedy was assassinated, Nov. 22nd, 1963, stays fixed in my memory as well. I was on my way home and anxious to watch my favorite television show only to realize that every channel was reporting on what had happened in Dallas that day. The point is that when we call for our memory to return to the past, all the memories that come back to us, our first kiss, the death of someone dear to us, our first day in school, or the celebration of an important event, have something in common; they are filled with emotions. What subject I taught on Sept. 11th, 2001, I do not know any more than what I was doing on the day of Nov. 22nd, 1963. Perhaps, you feel the same?

This means that any event that is emotionally charged is registered more strongly in our declarative memory. However, it is important to understand that emotions do not reinforce our memory in all situations. In the case of stress, for instance, the emotional reaction attached to it can impair the memorial performance[29]. Therefore, emotions can have either a strengthening or a weakening effect on memory and the learning process. Table 2.5 summarizes the effects of negative and positive emotions on the academic output.

Table 2.5
Impact of emotions on the academic output

Negative emotions	Positive emotions
Block	Motivation
Drop out	Interest
Absenteeism	Engagement
Waste of time	Perseverance
Sabotage	Collaboration
Procrastination	Flexibility
Resistance	Open minded
Awful communication	Compassion
Interpersonal conflicts	Acceptance
Lack of collaboration	Creativity
Insecurity	Harmony

How can we explain that emotions do interfere with the learning process? The main reason comes from the fact that emotions have a strong impact on perception, judgment, and behaviors. The key processes responsible for altering our mental faculties are very complex and beyond the scope of this book, for now let us say that they are biological and chemical in nature.

Let us go back to the six primary emotions discovered by Paul Ekman; fear, anger, sadness, disgust, surprise and joy. Of all these basic emotions, only one is truly positive and all others are negative, except 'surprise' in certain situations,

---

29 Phelps, E. (2000).

Emotions and their impact   45

and so generate behaviors that hinder the learning process. Flight, aggressiveness, withdrawal, and rejection are all behavioral reactions that are caused by negative primary emotions. As for negative background emotions, they have a much greater impact on cognitive and intellectual functions such as attention, perception, judgment, and, of course, the memorization process. We know that the activation of the amygdala is linked to the modulation of motor, cognitive, attention and memory processes[30]. Let us now examine the impact of our emotions on each of these functions.

Emotion and attention

Attention is not only the first link of the learning process but probably the most responsive to stimuli. It has been shown that emotions have an impact on the attention mechanisms, i.e., elements that have a negative charge have the ability to get our attention. To study this concept, a group of researchers developed an experiment where subjects were asked to identify an intruder among a series of neutral images[31]. The intruders could be a snake among flowers or a flower among snakes. Researchers discovered that the time it takes to detect the intruder that frightens (a snake among flowers) is less than the time it takes to detect a harmless intruder (a flower among snakes). See figure 2.1. In as primitive a context as the one in which our ancestors lived, we can easily imagine how these emotional reactions may have saved many lives. Indeed, thanks to the flight response, many of our ancestors may have survived the fear of a predator or a grizzly bear in the forest.

Figure 2.1 The average time it takes to detect a flower among snakes is 1060 milliseconds, while the average time it takes to detect a snake among flowers is 915 milliseconds.

And this does not only apply to images of snakes. It appears that it also applies to any situation that can potentially represent a threat to us. For instance, the same phenomenon occurs when it comes to identifying people with a threatening expression. Take a close look at figure 2.2. Perhaps you have not noticed but of all the neutral faces on the right, your brain was quicker at identifying the spiteful face than it was at identifying the smiley face among all the neutral faces on the left.

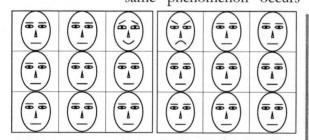

Figure 2.2 The average time it takes to detect a smiley face among neutral faces is greater (1600 milliseconds) than the average time it takes to detect a threatening face among neutral faces (1500 milliseconds). It takes even less time for people who are uneasy in society.

It is almost as if we were biologically programmed to more easily and rapidly detect the negative than the positive. Further, when you saw the image of the aggressive face, you reacted and your body went to an activation mode, prepared to deal with a potential aggressor. Your heart rate slightly increased, your adrenals secreted adrenaline and your muscles

---

30 Dolan, R.J. (2002).
31 Öhman, A. (2001).

Chapter 2

somewhat tightened. Then, in the absence of a threat, your body returned to normal. All these reactions are unconscious in that they take place spontaneously, extremely rapidly and by way of our reflexes. What is more interesting is that if you are a person who lives an uneasy life, the time it will take you to detect the threatening face among the neutral faces is much less and your physiological reactions will be more intense. Moreover, if you return to the photos of the six primary emotions in the beginning of this chapter, you will, on average, spend more time looking at the negative emotions as opposed to the positive one.

By being mindful of these scientific studies on emotions, I became aware of a reflex that I have when I give a workshop or a class. When I am in front of people I am not acquainted with my first reaction is to isolate people in the group who could represent a threat to me. How? By relying on their facial expressions and traits I can detect those who strike me as the most aggressive or unpleasant. This behavior allows me to modify my attitude towards them. In other words, I prepare myself to the possibility of having to "tame" them simply because I feel that they may disrupt my class. My approach is more targeted at integrating these students. At the first recess, I take time to become acquainted with them so that they become friendlier toward me and more pleasant in my class. Most of the time, the results are good because most of these students now view me in a more positive and favorable light. Similarly, my view of them has changed as well. The opposite is also true. Students who smile and who are pleasant have a reassuring effect on me and I rely on them tremendously in the beginning of my class, taking comfort in their allegiance. I realized that this unconscious reflex that I developed could be different in other people. Indeed, I have noticed in some teachers that if a student looked unpleasant or aggressive it was enough to trigger in them a hostile or even confrontational behavior. It is as though they were unconsciously conditioning themselves to confront the student that their emotional brain identified as a potential 'opponent'.

Our brain is programmed to react to any signs that could represent a potential threat for us. And five out of six emotional reactions ensure that this kind of reaction takes place.

The link between emotions and the learning process becomes evident. Each time that our attention is monopolized by a negative emotional charge, our learning and performance are affected. As Daniel Goleman explains : "emotions that have a strong negative charge, and the activities linked to them, attract our attention and ensure that it does not shift elsewhere[32]". For a long time, we have noted that difficulties with learning existed in anxious and stressed out people. Bettina Seipp has carried out a meta-analysis of publications dealing with the effects of anxiety on academic performance[33]. She made a list of 126 studies linked to 36 000 students. The outcome was that the more a student worried the less he was successful in school irregardless of the reference criterion; annual

---

32 Goleman, D. (1995).
33 Seipp. B. (1991).

Emotions and their impact   47

average, mid- or end-of-term exams, et cetera. Yet, it is only recently that we began to highlight the underlying mechanisms linked to this phenomenon. Indeed, researchers have determined that the attention processes could be the first ones to be affected by stress and anxiety. This would explain that any kind of performances can be diminished by our negative emotions[34].

Emotion and perception

Another important aspect is the impact that our emotions have on our perception. All our emotions act on our perception differently. For instance, we know that an emotional charge has a negative impact on our peripheral vision. It has been demonstrated that the ability to perceive peripheral information was deeply compromised in anxious subjects[35]. In other words, our perception is limited when we experience negative emotions. Consequently, if information is missing, our memory and learning process are directly affected. This phenomenon is well explained by David Rudrauf : "we know that a euphoric feeling enables us to concentrate on success whereas stress and anxiety have an opposite effect, i.e., they enable us to focus more on danger[36]."

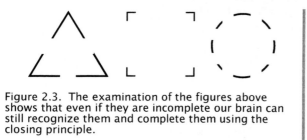

Figure 2.3. The examination of the figures above shows that even if they are incomplete our brain can still recognize them and complete them using the closing principle.

Another phenomenon linked to emotions has to do with the plain alteration of perception. This alteration can either consist of ignoring information presented in our perceptual field or adding information that simply does not exist. In psychology, there exists a very simple and well-known perceptual phenomenon called "closing" that can help us understand the alteration mechanisms of our perception by our emotions. The phenomenon is involved in completing an incomplete form, as shown in the few examples of figure 2.3.

B 12 13 14
A B C

Figure 2.4 If you look at the image on the left and you are asked to spontaneously say what you see, 50 percent of people will say the number 13 and 50 percent of people will say the letter B. But if we modify the context (figure on the right), the perceptions are directly influenced by it.

The 'closing' phenomenon, which consists of completing the missing links, is easy to understand. We can also understand how useful it is when we have incomplete information. However, depending on the context, it is possible to misinterpret the information, as shown on figure 2.4.

In fact, the principles that explain the phenomenon described above simply have to do with the perception and interpretation of shapes. When it comes to perceiving a more complex reality, however, not only do our previous experiences interfere but our emotions do as well. Let us take a very simple example. Imagine that you get

34 Janelle C.M. (2002).
35 Shapiro K. L, Lim A. (1989).
36 Rudrauf, D. (2003).

Chapter 2

home from work earlier than usual and that a sports car is parked in the driveway. You decide to look through the window to see what is happening inside. Then you see your spouse jumping in a man's arms after receiving a bouquet of flowers from him. Just as you did with the incomplete triangle, circle, or square from the figure above you immediately complete the missing links of the situation. The context will surely influence you no doubt but your emotions have a considerable impact on your perception. This perception has been induced by different things; the sports car, the man with the bouquet of flowers, and your spouse who jumps into his arms. As the emotions rise, your entire perception and interpretation processes start to become affected. In fact, your chances of reaching completely erroneous conclusions are very high. The majority of people see the number 13 when it is placed between two numbers, and the letter B when between two letters. Here, the majority of people see a woman in the arms of her lover. But in reality, he is a television host who came to deliver the car that she had won in a television contest. And, of course, her spontaneous reaction is to jump into his arms.

If emotions can considerably alter our perception as we have just seen, they can, therefore, affect our judgment.

Emotion, working memory and problem solving

It is noteworthy that the working memory is linked to short-term memory and allows to carry out most of the explicit cognitive tasks. We can compare it to our desk where we put the objects and tools required to accomplish a task. Its space and duration are limited. Thus, we can easily understand that anything that unnecessarily clutters up our working memory can potentially affect its efficiency. Many studies have highlighted the fact that emotions negatively affect the treatment of information in our working memory[37]. In particular, it was discovered that cortisol was secreted in stressful situations. Therefore, subjects with the highest levels of blood cortisol completed less mental arithmetic tasks than subjects with lower levels[38]. Other studies have shown that the pressure caused by the time factor had a considerable effect on the arithmetic performance[39]. It was also shown that students who feared mathematics lacked the ability to suppress anything that could potentially distract them. This deficiency of the inhibition mechanisms leads to a consumption of the working memory resources via all sorts of distractions that have nothing to do with the task[40].

Emotion, judgment and reasoning

With the case of Elliot earlier, we saw the extent to which the absence of emotions could affect the decision making process. But the reverse is also true. An emotional charge that is too intense can affect the complex cognitive processes such as judging and reasoning. A very original experiment has

37 Terry W.S., Burns J.S. (2001).
38 al'Absi M, Hugdahl K, Lovallo W.R. (2002).
39 Kellogg J.S., Hopko D.R., Ashcraft M.H. (1999).
40 Hopko D.R., Ashcraft M.H., Gute J., Ruggiero K.J., Lewis C. (1998).

demonstrated this phenomenon[41]. Researchers asked 170 subjects to read violent cartoons. Half of the group had to read extremely violent cartoons while the other half was asked to read less violent cartoons. And so, all the participants had to read five hypothetical stories concerning children having an aggressive attitude toward other children, without knowing the purpose of the study. Then, participants had to answer questions regarding the intentions of the researchers, their reprisal potential, and their emotional state. Results showed that the subjects who read extremely violent cartoons attributed more hostile intentions, more reprisals, and more negative emotional states to the instigators than the subjects who read less violent cartoons. We can therefore conclude that their negative emotions played a huge role in affecting their judgment and their ability to evaluate the situation.

When our emotional level reaches a certain threshold our intellectual and cognitive abilities are greatly reduced as a result. An interesting study has highlighted the negative impact of anxiety on a reasoning task[42]. One hundred and two subjects were given the task of solving one hundred geometrical analogies under two different conditions, non-stressful or stressful. The response time and the number of mistakes were calculated. Results showed that under the non-stressful condition, the most anxious subjects were slower and less accurate than the less anxious ones. Under the stressful conditions, however, the most anxious subjects were faster but were making more mistakes than the less anxious subjects. The researchers' conclusion is quite interesting. They explain that under the stressful condition, the divergence in the results between the two groups is more related to the difference in the quickness-preciseness compromise than to the difference in cognitive abilities (treatment of information).

When our basic functions such as attention, perception, working memory, judgment, and reasoning are affected by emotions, we can easily infer their impact on the academic output. Indeed, an Italian researcher has observed that worries are the most critical emotional components affecting academic output[43]. Other researchers were also led to what is called "academic anxiety" in medical students[44]. They have discovered that academic anxiety was not only associated to first year performances but also combined with past successes. Another study has come to similar conclusions regarding stress[45].

41 Kirsh S.J., Olczak P.V. (2002).
42 Leon M.R., Revelle W. (1985).
43 Comunian A.L. (1993).
44 Grover P.L. & Smith D.U. (1981).
45 Stewart S.M., Lam T.H., Betson C.L., Wong C.M., Wong A.M. (1999). vol. 33(4), p. 243-50.

Chapter 2

Exercise 2.2
Flashback on my day at school

Instructions : Take a few moments to ponder on your day teaching at school. Describe a situation in which you reacted emotionally and try to identify the one or many emotions that you felt by using the table describing different emotions and by jotting down the intensity of what you felt. You can refer to the example of Jennifer presented in the exercise 2.1 and then explain how these felt emotions can have an impact on your cognitive and intellectual functions.

Example :
Description of the situation : *Jennifer is leading a workshop on communication. Someone's cellular phone is ringing a first time. Jennifer then reminds the participants about turning their cellular phones and pagers off. A few minutes later, the same cellular phone rings again. Jennifer raises her voice and warns him to turn it off. After a few more minutes, the same story again. This time, Jennifer demands that the person goes outside the room to answer his call. Affected by the situation, Jennifer has a hard time to resume her workshop.*

Category	Emotions	Intensity
		Little .... Very much
Fear	Affraid	
	Worried	
	Timid	
	Insecure	
	Bewildered	
Anger	Annoyed	(filled to ~70%)
	Irritated	(filled to ~75%)
	Frustrated	(filled to ~95%)
	Impatience	
	Angry	
Sadness	Bored	
	Disappointed	(filled to ~55%)
	Discouraged	
	Sorry	
	Sad	
Disgust	Bitterness	
	Humiliated	(filled to ~40%)
	Be reluctant to	
	Intimidated	
	Disgusted	
Contempt	Contempt	
	Discredit	
	Underestimated	
	Revolted	
Surprise	Astonished	
	Surprise	
	Amazed	
	Impressed	
Joy	Happy	
	Confident	
	Content	
	Enthusiastic	
	Optimistic	

Emotions and their impact

	Impact of emotions on cognitive and intellectual functions			
Emotions felt	Attention	Perception	Working memory and problem-solving	Judgment and reasoning
Irritation Frustration Anger	All her attention was focused on the person with the phone.	The sound of the phone ringing was resonating in her head excessively. The sound felt louder than what it really was.	She was frequently losing her train of thought while she was explaining.	She had a tendency to exaggerate the importance of that situation.
Deception	Her attention was also focused on the students who were sighing each time the phone would ring.	She started combining the slightest signs of impatience from the participants towards the person on the phone with signs of disinterest for the class itself.	She forgot 2 or 3 important aspects in her explanations.	She was no longer able to explain properly and clearly what she usually does very easily.
Humiliation	She started concentrating on everything that could disturb her.	When two participants started laughing, she felt they were laughing at her.	Her ideas were more and more confused.	Dark ideas started to appear in her mind.

Description of the situation :

_____

_____

_____

Category	Emotions	Intensity	
		Little	Very much
Fear	Affraid-------------		
	Worried------------		
	Timid-------------		
	Insecure ------------		
	Bewildered ---------		
Anger	Annoyed------------		
	Irritated------------		
	Frustrated-----------		
	Impatience----------		
	Angry--------------		
Sadness	Bored---------------		
	Disappointed--------		
	Discouraged--------		
	Sorry---------------		
	Sad-----------------		
Disgust	Bitterness-----------		
	Humiliated----------		
	Be reluctant to------		
	Intimidated---------		
	Disgusted-----------		
Contempt	Contempt-----------		
	Discredit------------		
	Underestimated-----		
	Revolted------------		
Surprise	Astonished----------		
	Surprise------------		
	Amazed-------------		
	Impressed----------		
Joy	Happy---------------		
	Confident-----------		
	Content-------------		
	Enthusiastic---------		
	Optimistic----------		

	Impact of emotions on cognitive and intellectual functions			
Emotions felt	Attention	Perception	Working memory and problem-solving	Judgment and reasoning

Neurological mechanisms

Famous researcher Joseph LeDoux of New York University explains that the emotional system can have monopoly of all of our brain's resources[46]. It is as though emotions could take control over our entire cognitive and perceptual functions. This is why even from a minor event, our brain can create a fictitious scenario and will do all it can to reinforce a variety of hypotheses that will validate the way we feel. LeDoux explains that it is much easier for our emotions to take control over our thoughts than for our thoughts to take control over our emotions.

To be more precise, it is the amygdala, this nervous structure which is central to "our emotional brain" that emits neuronal projections to many parts of the brain including the ones responsible for higher cognitive functions. Conversely, the neural projections that come from these cognitive regions and go to the amygdala are more limited. This can explain why our emotions have such an impact on our behaviors and cognitions and why when they reach a certain intensity we can lose our control. We will see a little further that there are also downstream pathways that can be stimulated when it comes to emotion management. But for now, we will focus more specifically on the impact of negative emotions.

For a long time, reason and passion have been seen as different and diametrically opposed entities. Because reality is a bit more complex than this simplified duality, as described in chapter 1, there exist distinct cerebral structures to explain the functioning of cognitive (rational), technical, relational, and emotional competencies.

In general, when we want to "rationalize" someone who is being emotional, we talk and try to reason that person. But, more often than not, this method is futile because the emotional brain of someone undergoing an emotional crisis does not recognize language or words as the rational brain does. Indeed, language is the rational brain's way of communicating and functioning whereas the emotional brain deals more with gestures, behaviors, and actions. If we talk when we are angry, afraid or sad, it could be for two reasons because the rational and emotional brains communicate and complement each other; and a more pernicious reason, because the emotional brain has the ability to dominate the rational brain. To illustrate this concept we can take a rider and his horse as an example. Usually, the rider controls, directs and guides the horse but when the horse no longer responds for whatever reason, the opposite effect takes place in other words, the horse becomes in charge and controls and guides the rider wherever it wants to go. And the situation will remain as such until the horse starts to calm down. In the same way, when the emotional brain loses control it has the ability to take hold of the rational brain, taking rein, so to speak. The rational brain becomes hostage and powerless.

---

46 LeDoux, J. (2001).

When their limits are tested, emotional reactions can considerably alter the learning process. We all know, and this has been scientifically demonstrated, that stress can affect our learning. Furthermore, works of Dr. Douglas Bremner et al. have established that Vietnam veterans suffering from post-traumatic stress have an atrophied hippocampus compared to normal subjects[47]. The same type of observation was made on children who had been victims of intense stress over a relatively long period of time[48]. Therefore, intense negative emotions not only have the ability to alter the learning process but also to lead to a destruction of brain structures involved in the learning process.

Other functional considerations are necessary. A number of studies on what we call "emotional asymmetry" have allowed us to have a better understanding of the way emotions work. The works of Richard Davidson from Wisconsin University have shown that emotional states were lateralized in the brain[49]. We have known for some time now that cognitive functions such as language and logical reasoning are located in the left hemisphere of the brain while nonverbal, musical and spatio-visual functions are located in the right hemisphere of the brain. But it is only later, through neuroscience studies, that we discovered the existence of the lateralization of emotions. Davidson and his team have shown that negative emotions such as sadness, disgust and fear were lateralized in the right side of the brain while positive emotions such as joy and well being were lateralized in the left side of the brain. We know that the amygdala is involved in emotions and the asymmetry in the cerebral cortex is more concentrated in the prefrontal region.

It would be too long and uninteresting to describe all the experiments and observations that have led to discovering the lateralization of positive emotions on the left and negative emotions on the right. But simply stated, the first observations go back to the days when researchers noticed that patients with a cerebral lesion localized in the left prefrontal regions of the cortex often suffered from depressive symptomatology. Conversely, observations on patients who suffered from comparable lesions in the same region of the right hemisphere resulted in highly positive effects. Studies on the physiological activity of the brain, thanks to mental imaging techniques, have confirmed these observations. Therefore, we discovered that when negative emotions were induced on test subjects, their right hemisphere was activated as opposed to their left hemisphere when positive emotions were induced[50]. More recently, it has been demonstrated that depressive people not only showed a reduction of the activity of the left prefrontal region of their brain but also a reduction in the grey matter of these same regions[51]. Another study, on 56 children between 8 and 11 years old, has

---

47 Bremner J.D. (2002).
48 Bremner J.D. (2002).
49 Davidson, R. (1987).
50 Sobotka S.S., Davidson R.J., Senulis J.A. (1992).
51 Davidson R.J., Lewis D.A., Alloy LB, Amaral D.G., Bush G., Cohen J.D., Drevets W.C., Farah M.J., Kagan J., McClelland J.L., Nolen-Hoeksema S., Peterson B.S. (2002).

Chapter 2

revealed that those who suffered from anxiety showed a greater activity of the right prefrontal lobe compared to normal children[52].

Another important element that was brought up earlier was the key role that the amygdala played in regards to emotions and its very important connections with the prefrontal cortex. Joseph Ledoux, from New York University, showed that the amygdala sends projections almost everywhere in the brain including, of course, the prefrontal regions[53]. However, a much lower number of projections reach the amygdala. This can explain why emotions can have such a great impact on cognitions. It also means that the emotional system has the power to monopolize the brain's resources and that it is much easier for emotions to control our thoughts than the other way around[54].

Moreover, a new source of information from Richard Davidson's labs brings additional knowledge to Ledoux's research. Davidson has discovered that the number of projections from the left prefrontal lobes descending to the amygdala is greater than those coming from the right side[55]. In other words, the amygdala rules in terms of inducing negative emotions and emitting projections toward the right prefrontal zones. But as far as positive emotions, the opposite is true, i.e., the descending projections from the left prefrontal lobes toward the amygdala are greater in number and thus able to modulate it. Researchers have demonstrated that an increase in the activity of the left prefrontal cortex was associated to a decrease in the activity of the amygdala[56]. They discovered that when their test subjects were instructed to voluntarily lessen their negative emotions, a decrease in the activity of the amygdala was observed. Davidson suggested that the connections between the left prefrontal regions and the amygdala play an important role in the management of our emotions[57]. He maintains that these mechanisms can be responsible for the decrease in the intensity of the negative effects and their duration in people who exhibit resilient characteristics[58]. In addition, researchers have discovered that children with resilient traits also revealed a greater activity of the left prefrontal lobe[59].

* * *

In summary, we understand that negative emotions have a powerful influence on all of our cognitive and intellectual functions. Nerve connections that are regulated by the amygdala have ramifications that make the latter "the ruler" when an intense emotion emerges. Attention, perception, working memory, judgment and reasoning are all affected by negative emotions. We have presented several scientific facts that support this phenomenon and can attest to the fact that negative emotions are responsible for many difficulties associated to

52 Baving L, Laucht M, Schmidt MH. (2002).
53 Ledoux, J.E. (1994).
54 From Benson E (2002).
55 Davidson, R.J. (2001).
56 Davidson, RJ. (1998).
57 Davidson RJ. (2000).
58 The term 'resilience' refers to the ability to succeed in life, to develop oneself and be happy despite the adversities and negative experiences lived. See Cyrulnik, B. 1999).
59 See Davidson, R.J. (2002).

the learning process. Hence, it is not necessary for the emotions that are experienced by the learner to be intense and acute as primary and secondary emotions are. They can be more diffused such as background emotions. In fact, background emotions are the most present because they can last much longer and cause extensive damage compared to primary emotions. It is true that having a fit of anger or sadness can affect us tremendously but since primary emotions are normally short-lived, we can return to a "normal" state rather quickly. But with background emotions which can last hours and even days, our well being and cognitive functions can be seriously undermined. It has been known that mood disorders such as depression or generalized anxiety can have serious consequences to our health by destroying our immune system or creating lesions in our cardiovascular system or in our stomach[60]. More recently, we have learned, especially with the works of Dr Douglas Bremner, that post-traumatic stress syndrome generated lesions in the hippocampus, where the declarative memory lies. For this reason, it is conceivable that if deep traumas leave traces in the brain, the same could apply for less severe traumas such as the ones that students sometimes go through during their school years. Hence, if students are not given a minimum amount of emotional help to cope with their academic exams, negative emotional traces can register in their brain and ultimately affect their intellectual, relational and technical capacities. This is why we think that emotional pedagogy is equally important and it is essential for all teachers and trainers to stimulate positive background emotions with respect to the subjects taught as well as the simple fact of learning. We will see in chapter 5, how it is possible to achieve this.

---

60 For a more detailed description, see Chabot, D. (2000).

Chapter 2

Chapter 3

Emotional intelligence

T he long tradition of the psychology of intelligence has followed a purely cognitive path. Up until 1980 most theorists and researchers who have studied the definition and concept of intelligence have shared an opinion that can be translated into those terms; intelligence is what allows us to succeed in school and consequently in life. Let us succinctly look back in history and trace the concept of intelligence.

1905 : Binet and the intelligence quotient

In 1905, the Department of Education in France asked psychologist Alfred Binet to develop a test that would predict which children would struggle in school and which ones would do well. Binet then created a tool which would enable him to measure certain intellectual and cognitive aptitudes necessary to succeed in school. From this work, the phrase "intelligence quotient" or "IQ," entered the vocabulary and was introduced in the United States several years later. Binet's test would be modified and adapted to the American reality and would give rise to the Standford-Binet Intelligence Scale. This will lead to the Weschler Scales, the Weschler-Intelligence scale for adults and the Weschler-Intelligence scale for children. From this day forward, the intelligence concepts would continue to multiply and evolve.

1927 : Spearman and the "G" factor of intelligence

For Charles Spearman, if you are intelligent in one particular area it means you are intelligent in all areas[61]. Spearman presumed that there was a unique and general factor of intelligence that would group together all of the cognitive functions. He assumed that intelligence was a unique cognitive faculty that he called the "G" factor. This unifactorial model gave Spearman the notion that intelligence was composed of a general factor that would apply to all activities calling for intelligence at various degrees.

---

61 Spearman, C.(1927).

1938 : Thurstorn and the multiple factors of intelligence

Louis Thurston had a very different notion of intelligence. For him, intelligence was not unifactorial but multifactorial. According to Thurstorn, intelligence is composed of seven basic cognitive aptitudes that are independent from one another. Therefore, in order to be intelligent, it is necessary to have a good verbal comprehension and verbal fluidity, good reasoning skills, numerical aptitudes, associative memory, and good perceptive speed and spatial aptitude. If only one of these factors is weak, then intelligence will be affected. For instance, if someone is struggling to understand language or has memory problems then his level of intelligence will be directly impacted.

1983 : Gardner and the multiple intelligences theory

For Howard Gardner, there are many types of intelligence and not just one. His observations have allowed him to distinguish eight forms of intelligence; musical, kinesthetic, mathematico-logical, linguistic, spatial, naturalistic, interpersonal and intrapersonal[62]. In Gardner's multiple intelligences theory, we see that personal and social aspects are taken into consideration. We will see further on that the concepts of interpersonal and intrapersonal intelligence developed by Gardner are conducive to the concept of emotional intelligence.

1988 : Sternberg and the triarchic theory of intelligence

For Robert Sternberg, the cognitive and intellectual processes that allow us to solve problems are more important than the right answers given in an intelligence test[63]. With this in mind, Sternberg developed a theory called triarchic intelligence, i.e., one that describes three aspects of intelligence; (1) the internal elements of intelligence which represent all of the mental processes that we use to acquire knowledge and solve problems; (2) the adaptative intelligence which we use to adapt or modify our environment or to chose new environments that are more compatible with our goals; (3) the intelligence resulting from acquired experience which consists of taking advantage of our life's experiences to accomplish tasks and to solve new problems.

1990 : Salovey and Mayer, from cognitive to emotional intelligence

Howard Gardner's and Robert Sternberg's greater insights have led Peter Salovey and John Mayer to the concept of emotional intelligence. They have come to the understanding that despite Gardner's and Sternberg's receptivity to greater intellectual realities, which particularly include personal and social elements, another dimension that could not be perceived within the traditional cognitive paradigm was lacking. Hence, Salovey and Mayer removed themselves from their predecessor's paradigm and came to the conclusion that emotions could not be ignored when the topic of intelligence was being addressed. And thus, in 1990 they developed a new form of intelligence called emotional

---

62 Gardner, H. (1983).
63 Sternberg, R. (1988).

intelligence[64]. Consequently, they describe emotional intelligence as : *"Our ability to monitor and regulate our feelings and those of others, to differentiate them, and use them to guide our thoughts and actions"*.

Yet the concept of emotional intelligence really became known to the public in 1995, thanks to Daniel Goleman's bestseller entitled "Emotional Intelligence, why it matters more than IQ". Based on Salovey and Mayer's definition in 1990,

Goleman defines emotional intelligence as : *"Our ability to recognize our own feelings and those of others, to motivate ourselves, and to manage our internal emotions as well as those involved with others"*.

In 1997, Salovey and Mayer revised and clarified their definition of emotional intelligence[65]. Emotional intelligence has become : *"Our ability to perceive, appreciate and accurately express our emotions; our ability to access and/or generate feelings when they ease our thoughts; our ability to understand emotions and emotional knowledge; and our ability to manage our emotions to promote emotional and intellectual growth"*.

As for me, it was while editing a work intended for college students and entitled Emotions and adaptation[66] in 1996 that I became aware of the concept of emotional intelligence. I then decided to write a book on the subject and tried to make the highly interesting yet relatively arid concepts of Salovey and Mayer more palatable. As a result, in 1998 I published a book entitled "Foster your emotional intelligence[67]." Later, I realized that I was the first French author to publish a book on this subject. Following several requests to be more involved in this topic, a sentiment echoed in my teaching environment, and in 1999 I founded the Society for the Development of Emotional Intelligence (SDEI), which has been renamed, the Academy of Pleasurology and Emotional Intelligence (APEI) in 2004, which focuses more on the importance of pleasure and emotional intelligence. And recently, specifically to to go thoroughtly into the topic of this book, we founded the Emotional Pedagogy Institute (EPI) so as to offer professional training on emotional pedagogy[68].

---

64 Salovey, P. & Mayer, J.D. (1990).
65 Mayer, J. D. & Salovey, P. (1997).
66 Chabot, D. (1996).
67 Chabot, D. (1998).
68 See www.emotionalpedagogy.com

Table 3.1
Evolution of the concept of intelligence

Year	Researcher	Concept of intelligence
1905	Alfred Binet	What allows us to succeed in school
1927	Charles Spearman	Unique general cognitive aptitude
1938	Louis Thurnston	Composed of seven independent factors
1983	Howard Gardner	Eight different forms of intelligence
1988	Robert Sternberg	Three distinct elements
1990	Peter Salovey and John Mayer	Emotional intelligence : a non-cognitive form of intelligence
1996	Daniel Goleman	Emotional intelligence : what enables us to succeed in life

Our definition of emotional intelligence

We have tried our best to respect Peter Salovey and John Mayer's vision as much as possible. For us, emotional intelligence is a collection of competencies allowing to :

- Identify our own emotions and those of others;
- Accurately express our emotions and help others express theirs;
- Understand our own emotions and those of others;
- Manage our own emotions and adapt to those of others;
- Use our own emotions and the skills peculiar to emotional intelligence in various areas of our lives in order to better communicate, make good decisions, manage our priorities, motivate ourselves and others, maintain good interpersonal relations, et cetera.

Let us examine, one by one, the five basic emotional intelligence competencies and try to understand their involvement in pedagogic strategies.

The identification of emotions

In order to understand how an emotion is identified, we must have an idea of what an emotion consists of. In general, we can identify five distinct components of an emotion :

- Nonverbal expressions (facial and physical) frowning, tight jaw, elevated shoulders, bulging eyes, et cetera.
- Physiological changes such as an increase in the heart rate and blood pressure, perspiration, dryness of the mouth, muscular tension, et cetera.
- Adaptative behaviors such as approach or avoidance, flight or fight, affection or aggression, et cetera.
- Thoughts that are also called "cognitive evaluations" and that deal with actual life experiences. These thoughts help to have an idea of what is happening, determine if there is danger, or assess if the situation has any

ties with our values or belief system, et cetera. In fact, it has to do with the dialog one has internally when faced with a situation that generates emotions.

- Affective feelings that help identify and classify the emotion felt.

Therefore, when we feel an emotion each of the components described above comes into play and, because of these components we will be able to identify our emotions and those of others.

Our ability to identify our emotions and those of others comes very early in life. The identification of our own emotions is possible because of their physical and physiological expressions such as trembling when we are afraid, our heart that 'skips' a few beats when we are in love, or our voice that quivers and mouth that becomes dry when giving a presentation before the class. We must therefore be able to read these internal parameters with accuracy in order to identify our own emotions. Some people though are struggling at doing that.

The identification of others' emotions involves being able to read the observable parameters in the other person. We can rely on the tone of voice and the discussion but also on nonverbal expressions such as tight fists, frowning, elevated shoulders, or tensed muscles. And behaviors such as striking, withdrawing, or running away.

Studies on how to recognize emotions in infants indicate that this competence develops very early during their development. In their first months they stare longer at facial expressions of joy compared to facial expressions of other emotions[69]. Their ability to link an emotional state to a facial expression emerges around age three, with a certain accuracy[70]. It develops throughout their childhood and reaches a maturity when they reach seven or eight years old[71].
Another study has also shown that infants could decipher emotions by observing body movements. As early as age four, they can begin to decode body movements expressing sadness. At age five, they can decode sadness, fear, and joy whereas at age eight they can decipher all the emotions as well as an adult[72].

Based on some studies, the ability to identify emotions on faces varies according to age. For example, we have observed very few differences between children and adolescents[73]. Their competencies are relatively similar. However, a study comparing people from 20 to 40 years old with people from 60 to 80 years old has shown that older people were not as competent at identifying certain emotional expressions such as anger and sadness as younger people were[74]. It appears that the older we get the more we struggle to identify emotions and their subtleties[75].

---

69 Labarbera, J.D., Izard, C.E., Vietze, P., & Parisi, S.A. (1976).
70 Field, T., & Walden, T. (1982).
71 Gosselin, P. (1995).
72 Boone R.T., Cunningham J.G., (1998).
73 Lenti C, Lenti-Boero D, Giacobbe A. (1999).
74 Phillips L.H., MacLean R.D., Allen R. (2002).
75 Malatesta C.Z., Izard C.E., Culver C., Nicolich M. (1987).

This emotional competence is also linked to the ability to distinguish the expression of a "real" emotion, a mimicked emotion, or a hidden emotion. For instance, the expression of a child who wants something and who mimics sadness while hiding his true facial expression because he is lying, the expression of a student who cheats during an exam but pretends he is concentrating by looking at the ceiling, or the expression of a student who acts as if he understands what you are teaching but in reality is totally confused. The ability to detect lies is something very difficult to acquire. Past research demonstrated that people were usually lucky when trying to identify a person who is lying even when clues on the person's face and voice were obvious[76] until famous researcher Paul Ekman and his colleagues made a stunning discovery. They asked themselves if people affected by aphasia (inability to use or understand language) were better at detecting lies. An experiment was then conducted to verify this hypothesis and, remarkably, they discovered that aphasic people were significantly better at detecting lies from nonverbal emotional clues than people having no such language deficit[77].

Finally, other studies have shown that delinquent adolescents were less competent at identifying the emotional state of another person[78].

The expression of emotions

This emotional competence has two aspects; the one of expressing our own emotions and the one of helping others to express theirs.

Therefore, the expression of emotions is only possible if we have identified them beforehand. It seems trivial but many people have a hard time acknowledging their emotions and more so expressing them. And at the same time many people struggle to identify the way other people feel. We have already seen that identifying others' emotions is difficult to do in some cases. But the ability to help them express their emotions is as difficult if not more. One by one, let us look at these two aspects of the "expression of emotions" competence.

Expressing our own emotions and feelings with precision and relevance. Many people try to conceal their emotions and as a result struggle to put their feelings into words. Not only can these difficulties affect their ability to manage their emotions but also the fact that they are not verbalizing them can lead to health problems. For example, people who are able to verbalize their emotions following a traumatizing experience, either by talking or writing, improve their physical health, strengthen their immune system, and have less frequent visits to their doctors[79]. The opposite has been observed with people who are unable to express their feelings. They suffer from alexithymia (a condition where a person is unable to describe emotions in words) which has been linked to an array of

---

76 Ekman, P. (1996).
77 Etcoff N.L., Ekman P., Magee J.J., Frank M.G. (2000).
78 Savitsky J.C., Czyzewski D. (1978).
79 Berry D.S., Pennebaker J.W. (1993).

Chapter 3

physical and mental health problems. It is noteworthy that these people also struggle to recognize emotions expressed by others, whether they be verbal or nonverbal[80].

Helping others to express their emotions and needs. Here lies an important key to communication; learning to accurately decipher the language of emotions. This is important because in order to communicate properly we must be able to read emotional expressions correctly; be able to perceive the way the other person feels and put ourselves in their shoes to figure out their emotions and their underlying needs. Only then can we help them express their emotions properly. This emotional competence is called 'empathy'.

Previously, we have observed that children around the age of two who were able to recognize their own image in front of a mirror were more inclined to show signs of assistance to someone in need. The ones who did not recognize their image remained apathetic to a person in need81. These results go hand in hand with those suggesting that empathy is a factor that absolutely needs to be present when helping someone in need[82].

A study made up of students considered as "difficult to manage[83]" has shown that in addition to having anti-social traits and aggressive behaviors they were less empathetic than "normal" students[84]. Interestingly, researchers have also observed that these students were equally competent in understanding interpersonal problems. This observation seems important because it allows, once more, to demonstrate the difference between a cognitive competence (understanding interpersonal relations and its precepts) and an emotional competence (showing empathy and kindness towards others).

Another study conducted using 1011 children has shown that those who were the most apt at deciphering nonverbal signs were the most liked, psychologically stable, and had better scores at school than children who struggle to decipher nonverbal signs[85]. An interesting fact was that these children did not have a higher IQ than the others.

Numerous studies have highlighted the role of empathy in teachers. We have seen, in particular, the extent to which an empathetic behavior could stimulate students' autonomy[86]. Another example is a study made using 615 students in which it was shown that teachers' empathetic behaviors promoted a more significant learning experience in their students[87].

---

80 Lane R.D. Sechrest L., Reidel R., Weldon V, Kaszniak A, Schwartz G.E. (1996).
81 Bischof-Kohler D. (1994).
82 Reynolds W.J., Scott B. (1999).
83 The english term to designate these kinds of children is 'difficult to manage'.
84 Hughes C., White A., Sharpen J., Dunn J. (2000).
85 Nowicki S., Duke M. (1989).
86 Assor A, Kaplan H, Roth G. (2002).
87 Coffman, Stephan L. (1981).

Understanding emotions

According to Peter Salovey and David Sluyter, this competence is much more cognitive than the others[88]. They explain that the understanding of emotions involves several aspects :

Understanding the subtleties of emotionally charged words and their meaning. As seen in chapter 2, there exists an array of terms that qualify as emotional states. These terms can discern different emotions such as fear, anger, sadness, et cetera, and can also, when part of a same class of emotions, differ slightly from one another in intensity. For instance, doubt, worry, fear, and panic are all emotions registered in the 'fear' category yet they all express important variants. Also, depending on the context, there exist different meanings to a same emotionally charged word. As an example, there are different ways to use the word 'love;' loving to take a bath, loving to drink champagne, loving our neighbour, or loving our spouse or partner. These subtleties are cognitive, a priori, yet can have a huge impact on our interpersonal relationships, our communication with others, and our understanding of others. We saw earlier that empathy was a key emotional competence to help recognize which emotion others were feeling but it can also help others express their emotions.

Establishing the relationship between an emotion and its Trigger. In chapter 2 (see table 2.1), we learned that each emotion was linked to a precise Trigger. For example, sadness is linked to a loss, fear is linked to a threat, and anger is linked to an obstacle that interferes with the search for pleasure or the pursuit of a goal. Hence, when a person is afraid, we can understand that it is because he is threatened by someone or something. Likewise, when a person is angry, it is because an obstacle is preventing him from pursuing his goals, and when a person is sad, it is because he has experienced a loss. This understanding allows us to have a much more complete view of a situation. Therefore, a teacher, who perceives a student as being insecure or afraid when facing an activity or an exam, understands that the student feels threatened. Thus, he becomes better able to help him deal with this feeling and ultimately overcome it.

Understanding complex emotions. In chapter 2, we saw that there exist many emotions and that some are more complex than others. As explained by Robert Plutchik[89], primary emotions are like primary colors. When we mix them, we can create an array of other emotions. For instance, jealousy is a complex emotion composed of fear, sadness, anger, and disgust. Therefore, when we see a jealous person, we can recognize these different emotional states. This understanding allows us to see that we can, in a given situation but in different times, be controlled by emotional states that are completely opposite of one another such as love and hate in the case of jealousy. Understanding complex emotions also allows us to distinguish between primary, secondary, and background emotions.

---

88 Salovey P. & D. Sluyter. (1997).
89 See Huffman, K., M. Vernoy and J. Vernoy (2000).

Chapter 3

Understanding the transition between emotions. Our emotions are like the temperature; variable. So another aspect of this competence is to recognize that an emotion can pass through, adjust itself, change tone and even form. For example, sometimes we can be sad and suddenly become aggressive, or sometimes we can be sad and this sadness can progressively turn to anguish or anger. This understanding is of paramount importance because it allows us to adjust according to the emotional state of the person we are speaking with. If a student is demonstrating frustration when faced with a problem and while exchanging with him his emotion turns into deception because of his inability to solve the problem, then the teacher will have to adapt his approach according to this transition.

Management of emotions

There are a number of approaches that describe the management of emotions. In emotional intelligence, this aspect is very important and has, as for all competencies, an intrapersonal dimension (managing our own emotions) as well as an interpersonal dimension (helping others manage their emotions). Let us examine these two dimensions.

Intrapersonal dimension : managing our own emotions

The management of our emotions is emotional intelligence's fourth competence. It implies, at the very least, that the identification and understanding of one's emotional state has taken place. Emotional expression can also come into play if it involves a helping hand situation. Nevertheless, the management of our emotions will consist of intervening on each of the emotional components that were described when addressing the identification of emotions. As for us, emotional management is possible only if it addresses each of the emotions' components :

- The management of nonverbal expressions
- The management of physiological reactions
- The management of behavioral reactions
- The management of our own cognitions
- The management of emotional feelings

Management of nonverbal expressions

The management of nonverbal expressions involves facial and bodily expressions. The management of facial expressions rests on the facial retroaction theory. According to this theory, not only are facial expressions the reflection of the emotions felt by the person but, reciprocally, facial expressions can also cause, awaken or arouse emotions as well. Several studies support this theory. One of these studies involved asking professional actors to mimic different facial expressions on request and measure specific physiological parameters[90]. They discovered that when the facial expression corresponded to fear, for example, the actors' heart rates would increase and their body temperature would drop. In the end, facial expressions that are linked to the key emotions create

---

90 Ekman, P., Levenson R. W. and Friesen W.V. (1983).

physiological effects similar to when these emotions take place under different circumstances.

Another experiment consisted of asking two separate groups of subjects to hold a pencil in their mouths in two different ways while reading funny cartoons[91]. Subjects from the first group had to hold the pencil with their teeth only allowing muscles involved in laughter to be activated. On the other hand, subjects from the second group had to hold the pencil with their lips only ensuring that the muscles involved in laughter would not be activated and simulate a pouting effect. It is important to note that all subjects did not know that they were part of an experiment on facial expressions. Instead, they were told that the experiment consisted of measuring how handicapped people deprived of their limbs could feel. Then subjects were asked how they liked the cartoons that they had read. The conclusion was that those who were holding the pencil with their teeth found the cartoons very funny as opposed to the subjects holding the pencil with their lips.

In another experiment, subjects were asked to deliberately contract certain facial muscles during the projection of slides[92]. There were two possible expressions from these facial contractions, joy or anger. The slide presentation consisted of children playing together or members of the Ku Klux Klan. The purpose of this experiment was to assess if the "forced" facial expression from either emotion could intensify the subjective experience of the emotion that was linked to the images. Results showed that the emotional reactions felt when watching the children play were stronger in those contracting their 'laughter' muscles than in those contracting their 'anger' muscles. Conversely, the emotions of anger felt when watching scenes from the Ku Klux Klan were stronger in those contracting their 'anger' muscles than in those contracting their 'laughter' muscles.

Bodily expressions are also part of the nonverbal component of the emotions. If, for instance, you meet a strange person on the street, the fear that you may feel will come with several bodily tensions that only occur in a flight response. But if you feel anger, the fight response will likely occur. In the latter case, different muscles will be involved and tensions will occur at specific places in your body.

In short, just as for facial expressions, it has been shown that when a certain posture corresponding to a certain emotion is adopted, a subjective state linked to that emotion is induced.

As these studies show, the facial and bodily expressions of an emotion help intensify the emotional feelings that are linked to that emotion. The contraction of certain facial muscles sends messages to the brain, which are interpreted and involved in increasing the activation of the body. This activation will, in turn, lead to a greater emotional response.

---

91 Strack, F., Martin L.L. and Stepper S. (1988).
92 Laird, J. D. (1974).

Thus, the old adage "a smiling face always makes life more beautiful" has merit. The management of our emotions begins with a smile and a body posture brought forth by a positive emotional state.

Management of physiological components

The management of physiological components consists of responding to the physiological modifications that come with our emotional reactions. When we feel an emotion the physiological and corporal reactions that result come from nervous stimulations in the brain and from chemical substances (hormones and neuromodulators) that are secreted by various glands and the autonomous nervous system. Conversely, all these physiological and corporal reactions as well as the chemical substances released in our body will have an effect on the brain. This means that during an emotional reaction, our brain affects our body and our body affects our brain. All the corporal reactions that take place when an emotion arises are perceived by the brain. The same goes for chemical substances released in our body and returning to the brain through the bloodstream and specific nerve endings. In turn, these signals that are returning to the brain have an effect on it. Therefore, if we can manage to respond to the physiological and corporal components, we can directly feel the effects on our emotional reactions.

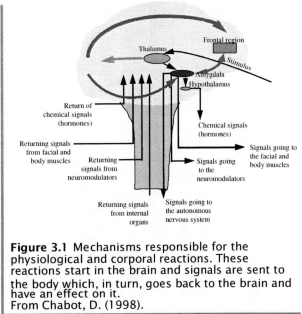

Figure 3.1 Mechanisms responsible for the physiological and corporal reactions. These reactions start in the brain and signals are sent to the body which, in turn, goes back to the brain and have an effect on it.
From Chabot, D. (1998).

Suzana Bloch explains that not only does each of the key emotions have specific facial and bodily expressions but a specific heart rate as well[93]. The latter is very important because it is possible to induce a specific emotional state by inviting the subject to reproduce its corresponding heart rate. This was, in fact, accomplished in an experiment where subjects were taught to reproduce the respiratory pattern of different emotions (see Fig. 3.2). At the end of the experiment, after recreating the emotional components such as posture, breathing, facial expression, and bodily tension, most of the subjects reported feeling the actual corresponding emotion.

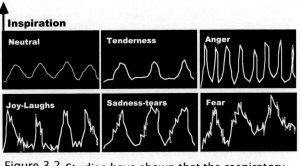

Figure 3.2 Studies have shown that the respiratory component of each emotion is characterized by the amplitude, the frequency, and the complexity of respiratory movements.
From Bloch, S. (1989).

---

93 Bloch, S. (1989).

Emotional intelligence

And the longer the experiment lasted, the more intense the emotion was. This experiment has shown that if it was possible to induce negative emotional states, it was also possible to induce positive emotional states.

Relaxation and meditation, two practices that gain more and more popularity, have shown to be excellent ways to decrease the harmful effects of emotions and stress[94]. These techniques help in reducing the physiological activation brought about by emotions. More precisely, it was discovered that meditation and relaxation decrease the activity of the autonomous nervous system[95] and lower the levels of stress hormones[96].

One of the fundamental principles inherent to all approaches used in meditation deals with the fact that everything in our body is interwoven. This unity spreads to many levels and represents an important part of our equilibrium. For instance, in our emotional plan there exists a true equilibrium between the physiological reactions of our internal organs and the proper functioning of our emotional brain. When we are upset, our physiological functions are affected; we have trouble with our digestion, with our sleep; our immune system is compromised, our thought processes are altered, we become forgetful, we lack concentration, our thinking is clouded, et cetera.

For several years, researchers have objectively observed this unusual link between the body and the mind. Antonio Damasio[97], a well known neuroscientist, formulated the "somatic-marker hypothesis," which explains how emotions are brain representations of body states; somatic-markers because these emotions are expressed through our body and guide our judgment as well as our reasoning, and may tip the scale one way or another.

Other researchers were able to highlight the unique connection that exists between the emotional brain and the heart. It is similar to a semi-autonomous neuronal network linking, what they call «the heart's small brain» to the brain itself (see figure below). This "heart-brain" connection is characterized by both organs interacting at every moment.

Of all the mechanisms that connect the heart to the brain, the autonomic nervous system plays a vital role. It is composed of two branches; one called 'sympathetic,' which accelerates the physiological functions of different organs including the heart and the emotional brain. The other branch, called 'para-sympathetic,' plays an opposite role by slowing down the functions of these organs. When the two branches are out of synchronization with each other, this can be compared to driving a car with one foot on the accelerator (the sympathetic nervous system) and the other on the brake (the parasympathetic nervous system) at the same time. Thus, "harmony" can only be achieved when there is a perfect equilibrium between the accelerator and the brake. There has to

94 Benson, H. (1975).
95 Jevning, R., Wilson, A.F. and Smith W.R. (1978).
96 Delmonte, M.M. (1985).
97 Damasio, A. (1994).

Chapter 3

be a precise balance or synchronicity between these two functions as we cannot press on both pedals at the same time. In our body, the same principle applies. A physiological synchronicity is necessary for the two branches to operate harmoniously.

Unfortunately, this balance can be compromised if negative emotions and stress take over and over-stimulate the sympathetic nervous system.

Thanks to sophisticated equipment, researchers have shown that when we are stressed and allow ourselves to be controlled by our negative emotions such as fear, anger and frustration, our physiological functions, particularly, our cardiac rhythm, become chaotic as shown on figure 3.3.

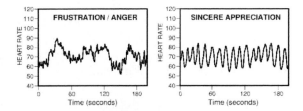

Figure 3.3. We notice that the cardiac variability on subjects feeling negative emotions is chaotic compared to the one from subjects feeling positive emotions. From McCraty, R. (2002).

Conversely, positive and benevolent emotions such as sincere appreciation, love and compassion are associated with a measurable cardiac coherence as shown on the figure below. This coherence reflects a synchronicity between the two branches of the autonomic nervous system discussed earlier.

This observation demonstrates that we can also induce this state of synchronicity and cardiac coherence through deep and conscious breathing exercises. The affects linked to the physiological and cardiac coherence are extremely fascinating. An erratic and disordered heart emits incoherent signals to the brain, which consequently inhibits our intellectual functions and limits our abilities to think clearly and to stay focused. On the other hand, a coherent and synchronized heart emits orderly and harmonious signals to the brain which, in turn, further improve its cognitive and intellectual functions. Therefore, people who practice developing a cardiac coherence not only feel less anxious, dissatisfied and angry, but also substantially improve their performance at work and at school.

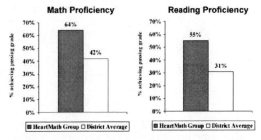

Figure 3.4. Percentage of HeartMath-trained students passing the Minnesota Basic Standards Tests in math and reading in April 2000, as compared to the district average passing rate for all seniors re-taking the tests at that same time. From R. McCraty, R., Tomasino, D., Atkinson, M. Aasen, P., Thurik, S. J. (2000).

For instance, a study carried out among 20 college students in Minnesota showed that those who practiced cardiac coherence (HeartMath group) improved their academic scores. Of the trained students re-taking the math test, 64% passed, as compared to the district average of 42% for all seniors re-taking the test at that time. The HeartMath group[98] demonstrated a mean increase of 35% in math scores and a 14% increase in reading scores on

98 McCraty, R. (2002).

Emotional intelligence

the Minnesota Basic Standards Tests. For reading, the trained group's passing rate was 55%, as compared to the district average of 31% (Figure 3.4).

Management of behavioral reactions

As described earlier, each emotion leads to certain behaviors such as flight, aggression, withdrawal, rejection, or irritation. So it becomes interesting to see how it is possible to modify these behaviors.

Physical exercising is an interesting way of acting on our behavior. Studies have shown that physical exercise and being in good physical shape reduce anxiety[99], stress and depression. It is possible, for instance, to improve these emotional states through intense physical exercises because of the increased production of endorphins and its anxiolytic effects[100].

Thus, the idea of reintroducing physical education classes in schools and encouraging teenagers to become involved in sports is in perfect harmony with emotional intelligence. Studies have indeed shown that sports' activities are positively linked to the emotional well being of adolescents[101]. Such activities allow focusing behaviors on things other than emotion-associated stimuli.

Management of our own cognitions

The management of cognitions has two parts : the first one directly addresses the management of negative thoughts linked to an emotional situation and the second one consists of managing the needs that lie underneath the emotions felt.

Management of negative thoughts

The management of negative thoughts consists of re-evaluating the situation and changing our attitude. It implies reconsidering and restructuring the thoughts that we nurse when we are emotionally affected by a situation. And even if we cannot change the situation, we can at least change the meaning that we give to it and, consequently, the emotional reaction that results from it. As an example, if we successfully avoid thinking about something threatening to us, then the anxiety linked to it will diminish. The same holds true if we can repudiate the idea that a situation does not correspond to what it should be.

The proof of the effects of cognitions on emotions has been highlighted in the 1960s in Richard Lazarus' lab. in Berkeley. Lazarus and his collaborators have conducted a series of experiments confirming that cognitions have an effect on physiological reactions of subjects that

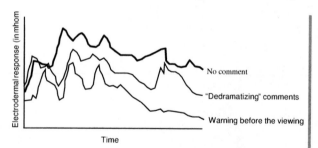

Figure 3.5. Electrodermal response during the viewing of emotionally-charged scenes with no comments, "dedramatizing" comments during the viewing, and a warning before the viewing. Adapted from Lazarus, R. S. (1991).

99 Morgan, W.P., and Horstmann D.H. (1976).
100 Colt, E.W., Wardlaw S.L.and Frantz A.G. (1981).
101 Steptoe A, Butler N. (1996).

were put through an emotional situation[102]. One of these experiments involved three groups who were asked to watch very painful images. The film was about a ritual among adolescents entering adulthood who, without being anaesthetized, were having their penis and scrotum deeply incised with a sharp tool. The first group watched the movie with no comments whatsoever. The second group was warned before the viewing that the film was going to show a safe and pain free medical procedure sought after by adolescents entering the world of adulthood. Finally, a third group could hear "dedramatizing" comments during the viewing of the film denying the traumatizing effects of the procedure on adolescents. During the presentation of these emotionally charged images, several physiological parameters were recorded including the electrodermal response[103]. Figure 3.5 summarizes the results of this experiment and shows that the group that was warned before the viewing of the film and the one receiving "dedramatizing" comments reacted less than the group receiving no comments. According to Lazarus, the information given to the groups helped to guide their cognitions and consequently modify their emotional state.

Management of the needs that lie underneath the emotions

Many people say that they react emotionally when faced with a situation because their values come into play. In emotional intelligence, there is no doubt that values are not the triggering elements of our emotions but rather our individual needs. For instance, if two people are having a discussion and they begin to argue, there is a good chance that emotions will rise. And if they are asked why they are arguing, they might blame it on the other for not listening, or not respecting one's point of view or beliefs, or lacking honesty or integrity, et cetera. In short, they will highlight principles and values in order to explain their emotions. The truth is that the reasons these two people are reacting emotionally have nothing to do with their values. If they are reacting, it is because their need to be right, to be highly regarded, or to be loved, for example, is threatened. Table 3.2 shows a list of values and needs.

---

102 See Lazarus, R. S. (1991).
103 The electrodermal response is a physiological measure which consists of recording the variations of the skin's electrical resistance under the influence of an emotion. When a subject feels an emotion, his sympathetic nervous system is activated. This activation causes the stimulation of the sweat glands and increases the hands' moistness. When the hands are moist, the skin's resistance decreases and, thus, favors electrical conductivity.

Emotional intelligence

Table 3.2
Values and needs

Rational and ideal values	Irrational and unreal needs
Love	To be right
Fraternity	To control
Equality	To be loved
Engagement	To be appreciated
Frankness	To have approval
Honor	To be perfect
Integrity	To be recognized
Justice	To be useful
Freedom	To possess
Loyalty	Power
Respect	To feel free
Responsibility	
	Security
	To be highly regarded

To summarize, our values are not the cause of our emotions. When our needs are threatened, they are the ones that activate our emotions. Our values only come into play after, to justify these emotions.

Values are simply abstract, rational, and complex concepts. They are the prerogative of the rational brain, are complex, and are maintained by the cognitive brain. Indeed, it requires logic and a well-articulated and structured language to be able to expound, explain, develop, and defend values. They are part of individual's ideals and also serve as a guide.

Conversely, needs are directly linked to the emotional brain. They are irrational, just as the emotions that they trigger are when these needs are irritated or threatened. It is said that they are irrational because they are often unconscious and very difficult, even impossible, to be handled by reason. In fact, imagine that a student is reacting to a remark from his teacher. And imagine that this student has an overwhelming need to be loved. If this student is asked why he is reacting, he will not answer by saying that it is because he is afraid to lose his teacher's love and acknowledgement. Instead, he will evoke values such as disrespect from the teacher or demonstrate his feeling of being victimized. It is said that needs are also unreal because no one and nothing can fulfill them. Indeed, nothing can fulfill our need to be loved, to be perfect, or to be right simply because they are impossible to fulfill. Yet the fulfillment of our needs seems to rest on other people, but these people also have their own needs to fulfill and can only focus on theirs.

The approach used to manage our irrational needs follows exactly the same path as the one used to manage our emotions. In emotional intelligence it is important

Chapter 3

to start by identifying our own emotions and the same approach must be taken for the management of our irrational and unreal needs.

The first requirement, for managing our needs, consists of identifying our irrational and unreal needs. When we react to a situation, we must ask ourselves what needs were irritated or threatened.

Then we have at our disposal at least three ways of managing our needs. In order to do so we must rationally confront our needs with the reality. For instance, the student who felt bad after being reprimanded by his teacher and identified that he feared not being loved will have to confront his need to be loved. He will have to tell himself that being reprimanded has nothing to do with not being loved.

The second requirement consists of finding a manner to self-satisfy our needs. For instance, the student will have to learn for himself to satisfy his need to be loved by evaluating all the reasons and all the people around him who love him.

A third requirement, for managing our irrational and unreal needs, is to detach us from them completely. When we become conscious that these needs are insatiable, because they rely on external elements that are out of our control, we understand that the only way to escape their influence is to detach ourselves from them. The way of detachment, introduced in almost all the great philosophies, definitely applies here, and instead of continuously trying to satisfy these insatiable needs, we must learn how to do away with them.

Management of emotional feelings

This part of the management of our emotions is fundamental because it is directly linked to our subjective state of well-being. In chapter 2, we talked about the notion of background emotions. As a reminder, background emotions have to do with a permanent emotional state that oscillates from well-being and quietude to all the irritable states that we can feel such as depression, anxiety, and worry. We also mentioned in chapter 2 that these emotional states were sustained by our prefrontal cortex (the right prefrontal lobes are associated with negative emotions while the left prefrontal lobes are associated with positive emotions).

The key element on which the management of background emotions rests lies on the functional asymmetry of the prefrontal lobes. In theory, works of Dr. Richard Davidson, et al., have shown that the descending projections coming from the prefrontal lobes to the amygdala caused a decrease in the activity of the latter[104]. They have observed a decrease in the activity of the amygdala in subjects of their experiment who were given the instruction to voluntarily reduce their negative emotions. And this was possible because of the activation of the left prefrontal lobes. In another study, researchers presented subjects with short movie clips filled with positive or negative emotions[105]. After the presentation,

---

104 Davidson, R.J. (1998).
105 Tomarken A.J., Davidson R.J., Henriques J.B. (1990).

subjects were instructed to rate their emotional experience during the viewing of the short clips. Subjects with a higher basal activity of the left prefrontal lobes felt more positive emotions to the positive clips than subjects with a higher basal activity of the right prefrontal lobes. It is noteworthy that this latter group had felt more negative emotions during the viewing of the negative clips. In another study, Davidson, et al., presented pleasant and unpleasant images to subjects[106]. The purpose was to measure two elements; (1) the intensity of the emotions felt by the subjects and, (2) how long their emotional state would last. Results indicate that subjects with a higher activity of the left prefrontal lobes felt negative emotions with less intensity and would recover faster from the effect of the negative stimuli than subjects with a higher activity of the right prefrontal cortex. Other studies have also shown that subjects with a higher activity of the left prefrontal lobes feel, in general, more positive effects and less negative ones than subjects with a higher activity of the right prefrontal lobes[107].

All of these results reflect a very interesting means of managing our emotions. Indeed, it seems that the best way to manage our negative emotions is to arouse positive ones. In fact, there is a great deal of scientific data to support this method.

The plasticity of our brain allows the creation of neuronal connections associated with pleasant emotional states[108]. By putting ourselves in situations where we can generate positive emotional states, we stimulate our left prefrontal lobes, and the neurons that are stimulated inhibit the amygdala thereby halting the flow of destructive emotions. By simply smiling deliberately it is possible to stimulate the activity of the left prefrontal lobes[109].

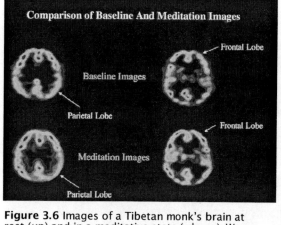

Figure 3.6 Images of a Tibetan monk's brain at rest (up) and in a meditative state (down). We notice an increase in the activity of the left prefrontal lobes compared to the right prefrontal lobes.
Form Newberg, A. (2001)

However, the most efficient way to activate our left prefrontal lobes is by practicing meditation. Dr. Newberg, of Penn State University, has made amazing observations by examining the brain of Tibetan monks at rest and in a meditative state. Figure 3.6 shows a clear difference in the activity of the subjects' left prefrontal lobes[110]. We notice that even at rest the left prefrontal activity is more intense than the right, demonstrating the long-term benefits of meditation. What is promising is that positive effects can also be obtained in subjects with no prior experience with meditation. Another experiment was conducted on scientists working for a biotech firm who suffered tremendous stress. The team was randomly divided into two groups. One was trained for eight weeks on a meditation

106 Larson, C.L., Sutton, S.K., & Davidson, R.J. (1998).
107 Tomarken A.J., Davidson R.J., Wheeler R.E., Doss R.C. (1992).
108 Davidson R.J. (2000).
109 Ekman, P. & Davidson, R.J. (1993).
110 See Newberg A, Alavi A, Baime M, Pourdehnad M, Santanna J, d'Aquili E. (2001).

technique focusing on living the moment. The other group, the control group, was on a waiting list. The electrical activity of the brain was then measured in subjects from both groups before and after the meditation training of the first group. Results showed that the meditation training could induce incredible calming effects. As expected, we noticed a lower activity in the right prefrontal lobes (responsible for negative emotions) and a higher activity in the left prefrontal lobes (responsible for positive emotions and for attenuating negative emotions) in subjects belonging to the group that was practicing meditation compared to the control group. Interestingly, these results were obtained after only two months of regular meditation practices[111]. Similar results have been observed by other researchers[112].

Therefore, positive emotions and pleasure have an extraordinary potential, not only to help us enjoy the moment but also to help us better react to the different situations in our lives.

Many scientific data relating the beneficial effects of meditation on cognitive and intellectual performances are currently available. Janowiak and Hackman have shown that the practice of meditation had positive effects on stress and self-actualization in students[113]. Another very interesting study was conducted on 90 children suffering from a slight intellectual deficiency[114]. Forty-five of them were trained to practice breathing, yoga (pranayama, sithilikarana vyayama, suryanamaskar, yogasanas), and meditation techniques for one full year. The other 45 students were part of the control and were grouped according to their age, IQ, socio-economic status, and social environment. None of them ever practiced yoga, breathing, or meditation. They were merely concerned with attending their classes daily. Amazingly, researchers observed a significant increase in the IQ and the social adaptations parameters in children who practiced yoga and meditation. Another study conducted on medical students has shown that the practice of yoga not only had positive effects on the stress levels experienced during exams but also on the output of these exams[115]. Indeed, students who had practiced meditation had a lower failure rate compared to the control group. More recently, the positive effects of meditation on intelligence and academic performance were shown[116]. Researchers have observed an increase in the confidence levels and a decrease in the anxiety levels in students. In short, meditation not only had positive effects on academic performance but also on the psychomotor and cardiopulmonary functions.

Finally, the positive effects of meditation, among medical students from the University of Arizona, have also been shown on several other parameters and results showed a reduction in anxiety levels, in depression and psychological distress, and an increase in empathy and spirituality[117].

---

111 See Davidson, R.J. (2002).
112 Aftanas L.I. Golocheikine S.A. (2001).
113 Janowiak J.J., Hackman R. (1994).
114 Uma K, Nagendra H.R, Nagarathna R, Vaidehi S, Seethalakshmi R. (1989).
115 Malathi A, Damodaran A. (1999).
116 Shah A.H., Joshi S.V., Mehrotra P.P., Potdar N, Dhar H.L. (2001).
117 Shapiro S.L., Schwartz G.E., Bonner G. (1998);

Interpersonal dimension : helping others to manage their emotions

All the studies from the previous section (management of our own emotions) can be implemented in our relationships designed to help others who are having difficulty managing their emotions. Anyone who listens and pays careful attention to others is empathetic and can be of tremendous help to others. Empathetic teaching, as described earlier, can provide exceptional support to students. It can help them deal with difficult moments, overcome a decrease in motivation, and unravel emotional blocks linked to certain class subjects.

The teacher will, indeed, be able to help students overcome their emotional blocks that hinder their learning and they can also help them manage their emotions tremendously. We saw, in chapter 2, that negative emotions can affect our learning process, by altering our cognitive faculties (attention, perception, memory, judgement, et cetera.). Therefore, the teacher has a very important role to play in his relations with students in order to help them identify, express, understand, and manage emotions that can alter their learning process.

Ultimately, and as we will see in the second part of this book, the teacher will be able to refine his rapport with the students and pay special attention to their emotions. For example, if a student complains that he does not understand a certain class subject, instead of only addressing his cognitive competencies to help him understand, the teacher will have to access the emotions that are linked with his difficulty. He will then help the student manage his emotions by inviting him to examine his physiological reactions such as his breathing when relaxing, his nonverbal facial and bodily expressions, and his behavioral and cognitive reactions. And, in the end, this will enable him to develop positive background emotions.

Using emotions and emotional competencies

One of the key roles of the emotionally intelligent teacher is to stimulate his students' emotional competencies. You may recall an important principle mentioned in chapter 1; the true learning process takes place when we feel and not when we understand. The teacher will, therefore, have to implement ways to allow the students to feel what they are learning. These ways will have to involve the stimulation of the left prefrontal lobes so as to maximize the students' emotional well-being. Consequently, the teacher will be able to enable and stimulate all of the students' emotional competencies mentioned in chapter 1.

In the same way our emotions can affect our intellectual and cognitive faculties, they can also improve our learning and make it more efficient and enjoyable. Chapters 4, 5, and 6 are essentially devoted to the integration process of emotional pedagogy in our teaching.

Shapiro S.L., Shapiro D.E., Schwartz G.E. (2000).

Chapter 3

Part II

Incorporating emotional intelligence in our teaching strategies

A s mentioned several times, the true learning process takes place when we feel more than when we understand. As shown in the figure below, there are two aspects to the integration of emotional competencies in the learning and teaching processes. The first, which will be addressed in more details in chapter 4, deals with the management of emotions that are harmful to the learning process. The second, who will be addressed in more details in chapter 5, consists of feeling the emotions that are favorable to the learning process. In chapter 6, we will tackle how to stimulate the learning process in relation to the personality profile of the learner.

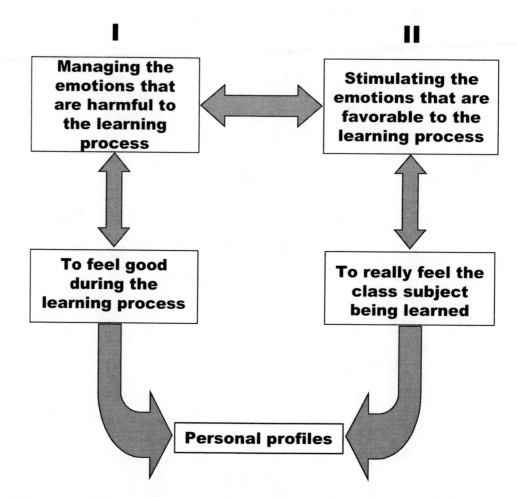

Diagram illustrating both aspects of the integration of emotional competencies in the learning process.

Chapter 4

Managing emotions that are harmful to the learning process

T he first condition required for learning is to feel good. This applies to everything because, as we have seen in chapter 2, negative emotions affect all of our mental processes from the most elementary to the most complex intellectual and cognitive processes. It is, therefore, evident that the learning process is very sensitive to the emotional state that the person learning is in. So teachers must recognize the importance of the role they play if they want to enable their students to learn. This is why they must, first and foremost, develop two essential qualities in order to be of assistance; empathy and compassion.

The power of empathetic and compassionate behaviors

Numerous studies have shown the positive effects of empathy and compassion. One of the most important of these studies was conducted by Robert Rosenthal of Harvard University[118] who has developed a test called PONS (Profile of Nonverbal Sensitivity). This test measures empathy through the use of a series of videos showing a person who displays various emotions. Scenes are recorded in such a way that one or several communication channels are suppressed. For instance, in some scenes the voice cannot be heard. Other scenes show only the facial expression while still others show only body movements, and so on. The role of the subject watching the video is to recognize the emotion displayed by the person solely by relying on nonverbal signs. This study, conducted with 700 individuals in more than eighteen countries, has shown that the ability to

---

118 From Goleman, D. (1995).

decipher emotions from nonverbal clues allowed individuals to better adjust their emotions to any given situation and to become more sensitive.

Other studies have been focusing on relationships. For example, researchers have compared what they call 'adjusted' couples to 'non-adjusted' ones. The adjusted couples are characterized as those who display a high level of empathetic listening and work to develop constructive solutions[119]. Firstly, they are asked to discuss, in turn, any two topics that deal with a current personal issue outside their relationship, i.e., work, health, and leisure activities. The one defining the issue is the 'plaintiff' and the one listening, the 'assistant'. The couple is alone in a room and their conversations are recorded on video. Then each participant is asked to watch and evaluate the discussion while each is expressing the issue and waiting for the other's response. This procedure aims at having every participant evaluate the quality of the assistance offered by the other when one expresses a personal difficulty. The individual doing the evaluation must identify all the verbal and nonverbal behaviors of the partner that were positive and negative. For instance, an assisting (positive) behavior is one allowing to clarify a discussion (example : "If I understand you correctly..."), to find solutions (example : "what would you think if we did this? "), or to feel understood and supported (example : "I understand what you mean" or "excellent idea!"). Nods of the head, supportive stares, and facial expressions of one of the partners can give the other the feeling of being supported. On the other hand, a hindering (negative) behavior, a negative statement (example : "Ridiculous!"), a refusal to deal with the problem (example : the 'assistant' always talks about him/herself or constantly changes subject), or a disinterested attitude (example : sighs, lack of eye contact, et cetera.), can be viewed as inappropriate interruptions.

As expected, those participants representing the 'non-adjusted' couples perceive one another as being less helpful and empathetic than participants from the 'adjusted' couples grouping. Conversely, researchers have observed that the participants of the 'adjusted' couples grouping pay more attention to one another than the participants of the 'non-adjusted' couples grouping.

American psychologist John M. Gottman has shown that the more a couple expresses emotional intelligence, allowing them to understand and respect one another, the more likely their relationship will be happy and long-lasting[120]. Gottman, et al., have conducted their research in what they have nicknamed The Love Lab. Hundreds of couples have entered this lab in more than sixteen years of research conducted there. In each case, they were asked to discuss a topic that they deemed significant such as money issues, children's education, or where their next vacation would be. All the conversations were recorded and as they were taking place several physiological parameters were also measured by researchers in order to detect the slightest physiological changes. Other parameters including body posture, facial expressions, and behavioral reactions

119 Cormier N. and Julien, D. (1996).
120 Gottman, J. M. et Silver, N. (2000).

Chapter 4

were also carefully analyzed. In conclusion, Gottman was able to predict 91 percent of the time which couples were going to get a divorce in the three years thereafter after only the first five minutes of listening to the conversations. Gottman emphasizes that a couple experiencing conflicts does not necessarily end up divorcing. The determining factor is the way the couple solves their conflicts. The more empathy and compassion the partners have for one another, the more harmonious they will be and the longer they will stay together.

Further, studies of couples have shown that the ones that are the least likely to stay together are those that are unable to detect nonverbal signs of emotions in their partner (facial expression, posture, tone of voice, gestures, et cetera.). For instance, during the viewing of a video, when an image is paused, and one of the partners is asked to interpret the emotion felt by the other partner at that moment, they are almost always awkward at correctly identifying the emotion. In other words, they do not see nor understand what the other partner feels. Consequently, when one does not feel understood, communication becomes extremely difficult, often leading to the disintegration of the relationship.

The same type of phenomenon can be observed with top management officials in a corporation. Those who are incapable of showing empathy and compassion are responsible for a fair amount of problems within the corporation. Conversely, empathetic managers usually have many advantages in terms of their rapport with employees. Goleman explains what these advantages are in those terms[121] : " *Empathetic individuals know how to 'hear' many emotional signals, which allow them to feel nonverbal emotions from a person or a group. They carefully listen and can understand the other person's perspective. An individual who has 'empathetic' skills will have no problem getting along with people from different backgrounds or from different cultures.* "

A study on corporate coaching has shown that empathy and consciousness of our own emotions were the two emotional competencies that distinguished the best managers and predicted their performance at work[122]. Richard Boyaszis, the author of this study, explains that empathy is a key characteristic to be able to understand a client, his goals, and his problems and condition at work as well as at home. Indeed, instead of seeing a client as a person entrusted with problems that can be distracting, the client is seen as a person who can learn new behaviors and skills. This is a fundamental point for us because when facing a student who presents difficulties with learning, we can focus on the situation and steer our assistance toward several tasks or exercises designed to bring the student to succeed in solving their own academic problems. But we can do better. We can look at the student and the emotional difficulties that he is faced with in connection to the learning approach that he is confronted with.

Interestingly, emotional qualities such as empathy and compassion are beginning to be studied in neurosciences. During one of these studies, Sean Mackey, et al., from Stanford University in California, have shown a series of videos to 14

---

121 Goleman, D., Boyatzis, R. & McKee, A. (2002).
122 Boyatzis, R. (2002).

Managing emotions

subjects[123]. The images presented to the subjects showed people suffering from injuries and pain. While the subjects were watching these images, their brain activity was measured using a scanner. When the subjects were not watching the videos, researchers placed an intense amount of heat on the subject's forearm and measured their brain activity while experiencing this pain. Mackey noticed a superposition of the brain activity in subjects who were both experiencing the pain themselves and also observing others in pain. Mackey explains that the sensation of pain and the emotion that comes with it are not two distinct components. In other words, they discovered an overlap in the areas of the brain that deal with the emotional component of pain and the areas responsible for the sensorial component of pain. This study allows us to understand that when a person feels pain and when we witness someone feeling pain, similar areas in the brain are activated.

A similar phenomenon as the one of feeling pain was discovered in connection to subjects feeling emotions experienced by others. In the brain, there are specific neurons that insure the identification of other people. Researchers call them "mirror neurons". Their role is to reproduce the sensations felt by people we are observing. Hubertus Breuer[124] explains that these neurons have a double function. On one hand, they perceive the pain and emotions of other people and, on the other, they simulate the feelings felt by others. Breuer adds that this mechanism can help learning through imitation.

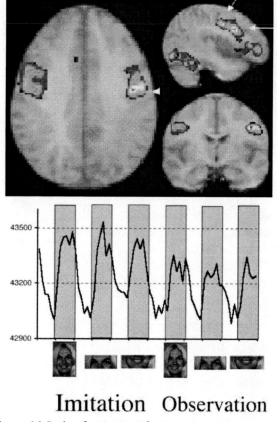

Figure 4.1 Peaks of activation of mirror neurons in a person observing another person who imitates an emotion.
From : Carr, L., Iacoboni, M., Dubeau, M.-C., Mazziotta, J.C., and Lenzi G.L. (2003).

Neuroscientist Marco Iacoboni, of UCLA[125] has shown that empathy can work through imitation. This can be seen in an experiment in which he invited seven men and four women between the ages of 21 and 39 to watch emotional expressions of joy, sadness, anger, fear, surprise and disgust. While they were watching, their brain activity was recorded with an MRI scanner. Iacoboni discovered that a specific neuronal network is activated when a person identifies or imitates an emotion. He explains that their discovery suggests that even if we do not openly imitate others, it is as if we understood their emotions through a sort of 'internal' imitation process. The regions in the brain that are activated when we identify another person's emotion are the same as those that are activated

123 McCook, A. (2003).
124 Breur, H. (2003).
125 Choi, C. (2003).

Chapter 4

when we feel this same emotion (see figure 4.1). The parts of the brain that are activated in those circumstances include zones responsible for physical movements (inferior frontal cortex and the superior temporal cortex) and zones responsible for emotions (amygdala).

Within the mechanisms that are specific to mirror neurons, some researchers have observed the basis on which all learning processes are grounded, i.e., observation and imitation. As far as we are concerned, mirror neurons play a significant role in the learning process because they are the ones that are activated when an external event takes place. Furthermore, it is our view that any pedagogue should seek the wavelength that connects him to the students by stimulating all the parts of his brain that will respond to what he is trying to impart.

Another fascinating discovery was made by Dr. Richard Davidson and his team. In chapter 3, we have discussed his work on how positive emotions were lateralized in the left prefrontal lobe of the brain. We then mentioned that people who engage in meditation practices could activate these zones in their brain. Davidson explains that compassion classifies as a positive emotion. Within the scope of a pilot project conducted on Tibetan monks, Davidson and his team have recorded the brain activity of one of the eldest members who had been cultivating compassion for more than 30 years. Remarkably, when this monk's basal brain activity was measured, they found that the activation of his left prefrontal lobe was the most dramatic of all those observed among a sample of 175 subjects[126].

All this data combined allows us to conclude that there is no doubt how empathy and compassion can, in their own right, contribute to the learning process (see table 4.1). As a reminder, in chapter 3, we have mentioned several studies demonstrating that empathy found in students and teachers had a positive impact on academic success[127].

126 Davidson, R.J. (2002).
127 See Hughes C., White A., Sharpen J., Dunn J. (2000); Nowicki S., Duke M. (1989); Assor A, Kaplan H, Roth G. (2002); Coffman, Stephan L. (1981).

Managing emotions

Table 4.1
Positive effects of an empathetic and compassionate teacher on a student

Positive effects of empathy	Description	References
Improves the ability for adaptation	The ability to decipher others' feelings from nonverbal clues allows a better adjustment of our emotions in a given situation and to become more sensitive.	Rosenthal, R., 1977
Improves the quality of relationships	Partners feel better understood and receive better assistance from their partner when he/she is more empathetic.	Cormier N. and Julien, D., 1996
Improves the resolution of conflicts	Empathetic partners are more able to detect the other's emotional signs and thus, can intervene more efficiently in their relationship.	Gottman and Silver, 1999
Improves communication	Empathetic individuals have no problem getting along with people from different backgrounds or from different cultures.	Goleman, D., Boyatzis, R. McKee, A. , 2002
Improves the perception of pain and the emotion of others	The brain of empathetic people responds to pain and the emotions of others in a specific way.	Mackey, S., 2003 Lacoboni, M., 2003
Improves the understanding of others' needs and difficulties	Empathetic people are better able, than non-empathetic people, to seize others' difficulties and problems and, consequently, can provide better assistance.	Boyatzis, R., 2002
Favors academic success	Empathetic teachers contribute to the students' academic success.	Hughes C., White A., Sharpen J., Dunn J., 2000 Nowicki S., Duke M., 1989 Assor A, Kaplan H, Roth G., 2002 Coffman, Stephan L., 1981
Stimulates the brain and favors positive emotions	Empathetic individuals show an increase in the activity of the left prefrontal lobe.	Davidson, R., 2002.

Exercise 4.1
The practice of empathy

Instructions : Below are the descriptions of three real-life situations experienced by students. After reading each one of them, try to answer the questions from the student's point of view.

Barbara's story
Barbara usually works very well. She is an ambitious student who dreams of going to medical school. She has good grades and participates with interest in the exercises given to her. She is curious and asks a lot of questions. But for the past two weeks, Barbara's attitude has seemed different. She seems disinterested by her class, often arrives late and, on the last exam, she scored lower than her semester's average. After a class, while she is putting her books away, you approach her and naively ask, "Is everything OK Barbara...? I have a feeling that you are less able to concentrate these days...". She looks at you, without saying a word, looks down and several tears begin to fall. She finally tells you that her boyfriend and she have recently split up, takes all of her things, and leaves the classroom.

Imagine that you are Barbara and try to answer the following questions :
What are your emotions?

Imagine that you feel the following three emotions : sadness, frustration and humiliation :
Why are you sad?

Why are you frustrated?

Why do you feel humiliated?

What reaction would you have liked to see from your teacher?

How do these emotions affect your personal and academic activities?

Managing emotions

Marc's story

Marc is a student with little discipline. He often arrives to class late and rarely returns his homework on time. He does not seem to care about succeeding. He has the bad habit of talking to his friends while you teach your class and then comes to you for explanations because he did not understand anything. When you ask him why he is always late and rarely returns his homework on time, he replies with a variety of excuses, leaving you to question his honesty every time you speak to him.

Imagine that you are Marc and try to answer the following questions :
How do you perceive your teacher's attitude?

How do you feel when you speak to your teacher?

Why do you feel this way?

What effects do these feelings have on your involvement and interest for your class?

What attitude would you like your teacher to have with you?

Steve's story

Steve is a hard-working student with a sincere desire to succeed. But he is struggling. He often comes to you and asks questions saying that he does not understand. Before each exam Steve comes to you with a list of questions that you already answered. From his questions you see that he does not understand a third of the class subject. Moreover, his answers to homework's and exams confirm this fact.

Imagine that you are Steve and try to answer the following questions :

In general, how do you feel about school?

Chapter 4

In general, how do you feel about yourself being a student?

What connection is there between these emotions and your success in school?

How do these emotions interfere with your understanding of the subject?

When you go see the teacher, what would you like to feel from him?

How could your teacher help make this happen?

Now describe a situation that you have experienced with one of your students.
Student's name : _____
Description of the situation :

Imagine that you are that student and try to answer the following questions :
What are your emotions :

Imagine that you feel the following three emotions; sadness, frustration and humiliation.
Why are you sad?

Managing emotions

Why are you frustrated?

Why do you feel humiliated?

What reaction would you have liked to see from your teacher?

How do these emotions affect your personal and academic activities?

In short, the integration of compassion and empathy goes through three steps. The first consists of detecting the emotions of the student who is struggling. The second consists of helping the student overcome his difficulties in an efficient manner. And finally, the third step essentially has to do with the second aspect (II) presented in the diagram on page 82, stimulating emotions that are favorable to the learning process. The first two steps will be addressed in the present chapter while the third step will be addressed in the next chapter.

How to detect the emotions of the learner

To detect the emotions of the person we are talking to, we must go back to the basis of communication; listening.

In chapter 2 we explained that each emotion has an Trigger and a subsequent behavior. The triad Trigger –> emotion -> behavior is fundamental. Although it is not always easy to detect the Trigger, in some cases it is directly linked to a situation. For instance, when a student does not understand an explanation and becomes upset, we can see the link between the Trigger and the emotion, i.e., it is a first-degree emotional reaction. Nevertheless, this frustration of not being able to understand can affect the student in one or many other ways. For example, he could be disappointed for not understanding, or fear the consequences of not being able to understand, or feel worthless for not understanding what others seemed to have understood easily. All of this emotional confusion will have important consequences on the student and his rapport with the learning process.

The role of the teacher will then be, firstly, to allow the student to identify, express, and understand his emotions and where they come from. But a very important phenomenon is likely to emerge in the majority of people; it is possible that it may be very difficult for the student to identify the heart of the problem he is experiencing. Since the problem is uncomfortable and painful, the reflex most people have is to refuse to identify what it is. Consequently, the elements mentioned a priori may turn out not to be the fundamental elements of the problem but rather those on the surface. The art of empathetic communication rests in extracting the fundamental elements of the problem; not to take the first elements that are mentioned at face value since they probably have nothing to do with the problem. Quite often it takes time to pinpoint the real problem or the real cause.

Since the real problem is painful, the student will try to protect his pain and will resist the idea of addressing it. Let us take the analogy of physical pain. For example, you hurt yourself while skiing and learn that you fractured your tibia. This injury will give rise to an inflammation that will turn into an oedema. The role of this oedema will be to isolate the injury and the swelling that occurs will "preserve" the fractured bone. The pain will then distribute itself concentrically around the fracture; the closer to the fracture or the real pain, the greater the pain will be. In other words, the inflammation surrounding the injury will be very painful but much less than the fracture itself.

Obviously, we know that the real problem is the fracture and this is where the treatment must begin. Therefore, if the focus is on trying to eliminate the swelling with ice and anti-inflammatory medication, then we will minimize a few symptoms but not treat the fracture, which is the real injury. Yet, the person with the injury will dreadfully oppose that anyone touches his fracture. Even upon examination by the doctor, the person will tense up in a reflexive manner and withdraw his leg in pain.

Psychologically, the phenomenon that takes place is similar. The closer we get to the real problem, the more painful it will be for the person to address the issue. Likewise, the "psychological injury" will be covered with a kind of "psychological oedema", whose role will be to protect the real injury. Thus, in the case of a teacher helping the student with learning or adaptation problems, his role will be to discover the real 'injury,' the emotional charge involved and how it interferes with the learning process. The key will be to remember that while peripheral symptoms can lead him to less significant problems, they may also guide him to the real problem.

In this context it is important to understand that the more painful it is, the more difficult it is for the person to expose his problem. The approach must be addressed progressively without being distracted by symptoms. The role of the teacher becomes the one of an assistant, a facilitator who will follow the student closely during the identification, expression and understanding of his emotions. Only then will he be able to help the student manage his emotions and succeed in his studie.

Managing emotions

The identification and the expression

In order to be able to understand and manage his emotions, the student must first identify them then express what he is living[128]. Although separate, these two steps will be addressed together here. As a general rule, the expression step involves three things; our experiences, our behaviors, and our feelings.

The expression of experiences deals with "what is happening". It is perhaps the easiest thing to express. Indeed, it is relatively easy to talk about our experiences because they don't really involve our emotions. We can talk about our life while remaining separate from our emotions. It is not unusual for a student to talk about his experiences. For instance, he can talk about his difficulties at school or about a certain teacher that he dislikes or about a test that he failed. In this case, his conversation will revolve essentially around his experience. The usefulness of expressing his experiences allows us to determine the problem's context and to have a general understanding of what the pupil is living. It also allows us to have an idea of what level and what sphere his problem is located at. However, since the expression of his experiences is superficial, the teacher's task will consist of helping the student go a step further by expressing, in a deeper manner, his behaviors and especially his emotions.

The expression of behaviors deals with "how he reacts and how he behaves". The pupil will not only tell what he has done or experienced, but also how he behaved under those circumstances. For example, a student says that last week he had three exams for which he studied all weekend. During that time, he encountered many problems, did not understand very well because it was difficult, and finally gave up after closing his books several times. This example relates an experience (the study of exams) as well as various behaviors such as when he closed his books several times, when he caught himself doing it each time, and finally, when he abandoned this act. The expression of behaviors implies that the person talks about his acts, attitudes, or his reactions. Compared to the expression of experiences, which can be impersonal, the expression of behaviors can be more intimate and more useful because it allows us to understand how the student acts or reacts in any given situation.

The expression of emotions deals with "how he feels". The individual expresses his emotions, i.e., how he feels or has felt. For example, if the student explains that he struggled with studying for his three exams, it is likely that he will also express how frustrated, angry, or sad he felt. This is precisely when we are getting closer to the fundamental goal of having the student express his feelings and emotions. To say what he experienced and how he behaved is only half the story since the expression of experiences and behaviors without the expression of emotions is like painting a canvas in black and white. The absence of emotions leads to the absence of many details and subtleties, like a colorless canvas.

---

128 Note that the pupil can express what he is living, what he is doing, and what he is feeling verbally as well as nonverbally.

Chapter 4

We know full well that the pupil will not necessarily express his emotions easily. Moreover, the first emotions that he will express will probably not be the deepest and the most significant ones. In the example of the fracture of the tibia, the more the emotions will be linked to the problem, the more painful it will be. In other words, the first emotions expressed by the student will be superficial at first and gradually become deeper as the process of identifying them continues.

A way to look at the identification and expression of emotions is to compare them with sedimentary rock strata. At the very top we see the expression of experiences, then the behaviors, and lastly the emotions, which will also be sedimented in layers ranging from the most superficial to the deepest. Thus, the art of empathetic communication consists of bringing the student to express his deepest emotions and to understand through this process what he feels within.

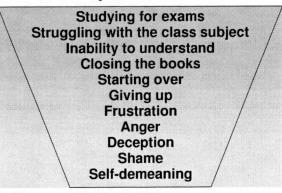

Figure 4.2 shows the example of the student who must study for three exams. In the beginning, he recounts his experience of spending the weekend studying and experiencing difficulties with the subject. Then he demonstrates how he behaved; did not understand the subject, closed his books, reopened them a few times, then gave up. Lastly, he taps into the expression of emotions and how he felt frustrated and became angry at first, then felt disappointed and ashamed, and finally, worthless.

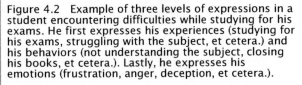

Figure 4.2 Example of three levels of expressions in a student encountering difficulties while studying for his exams. He first expresses his experiences (studying for his exams, struggling with the subject, et cetera.) and his behaviors (not understanding the subject, closing his books, et cetera.). Lastly, he expresses his emotions (frustration, anger, deception, et cetera.).

The understanding

The deeper the student gets in the identification and expression of his emotions, the more he will understand how he feels. In our example, he understands the situation at first, i.e., that the study of his exams is not easy, that he closed his books several times before giving up. He understands that his behavior (closing the books) is due to the frustration and anger that he felt. It is a reaction to his anger which itself is linked to the frustration caused by the lack of understanding. Then he realizes that he is disappointed, ashamed of himself, incompetent, and worthless. In short, as we progress in the expression of feelings and emotions, we unmask the person's real problem, which is generally tied to self-esteem and pride. What is also interesting is that the teacher can create links with him. Links between his emotional intensity and his confused state of mind, and how he may not feel intelligent or feel that he will never succeed in life, as a result.

Consequently, the student will ultimately understand that his feelings of shame and worthlessness have to do with all spheres of the problem evoked. He will feel worthless (devalued) because he does not understand what others seem to understand easily. But it is not easy to admit this because his pride will prevent him from doing so. Hence, it is for this reason that he will call on other emotions found in the primary category known as anger and aggressiveness.

These emotions of frustration and anger essentially protect him from the pain of having injured his ego. They are, essentially, the oedema around the wound. And the more he pays attention to his emotions, the further he will pass through these emotional strata and begin to deal with deception and shame (problems of self-esteem). We can, therefore, easily conceive that before dealing with the real problem linked to self-esteem and self-love, the student will go through these different strata that separate and protect him from the real problem, thanks to the defense mechanisms involved.

Here is when listening becomes a key element in order to help the student progress in the identification, expression, and comprehension of what he feels deep within. It is only at this stage that the door to the management of emotions will open and the teacher will be able to help him. Below we will first examine the different ways of listening (effective and less effective) and then assess ways that are more efficient. But first, we invite you to do exercise 4.2

Exercise 4.2
Listening

Instructions : Here are a few examples of dialogs between a student and a teacher. Try to spontaneously write what you would reply to the student.

Michael tells you, after receiving a bad score on his exam :

- I cannot believe this! I studied like a mad man for this test. I cannot understand why I got this score.
Reply :

Mary tells you, after you ask her why she still has not returned her homework:

- I tried to do it several times but I don't understand what I need to do. The instructions are not clear.
Reply :

You cross Paul in the hallway and he does not seem too happy. You ask : "is everything Okays Paul?"

- Well... I just walked out of a Spanish exam with Brown. He really asks tough questions. Everybody feel that they flunked his exam. In fact, the teacher warned us that the majority of students would fail. It's appalling!
Reply :

Carol pays you a visit at your office :

- I would like to have more time before returning my homework. I will have three exams next week and will not be able to do it. On top of it, I must go to my cousin's wedding.
Reply :

The different ways of listening

The emotional intelligence competency consists of expressing our emotions and helping others express theirs. It also involves relational and communication competencies; more specifically, actively listening to others in order to encourage them to express theirs emotions and not just limit themselves to facts, experiences, and behaviors. Unfortunately, very few people have transformed listening into an art. We will see how the majority of people listen and have an idea of why their ways of listening is often ineffectual at really helping others. Let us first examine the inefficient ways of listening in order to help.

The compassionate support

In general, people who do not know how to help have the reflex of offering their support when they are told about a problem. Often times, this reaction is linked to too much compassion. Indeed, the one who listens identifies himself with the other's problem and reacts exactly as he would want others to react if he were in the same situation. It is his own way of contributing and he believes that he is helping by reacting this way. For instance, he may try to comfort someone who is crying, reassure someone who is afraid, calm down someone who is upset, or cheer up someone who is depressed. This is indeed a common reflex to offer our shoulder when someone is crying or to tell someone who is afraid that there is no problem.

The person who offers support is generally very uncomfortable with situations involving someone else's emotions. In one extreme, he can trivialize the other's reality by simply giving that person a tap on the shoulder. Or in the other extreme, he can either cry with the person who is sad or become upset with the person who is upset. In this case, he is like a chameleon and takes on the other person's emotional color.

In this case, the person who brings support is not very helpful because, essentially, he is treating the symptom but not the injury, as with our example of the fractured tibia, by merely applying ice to the inflammation or casting the injury before disinfecting.

This type of support is compassionate but not empathetic because it is suffused by the other's emotion which may confuse the issue. Although, there are two possible scenarios; it is possible that the person who is assisted may feel understood but it is also possible that he may feel 'trivialized' by what he is experiencing.

Does this mean that we should never offer to help? Obviously not! But we must be sure that we provide support to the real problem or the real emotion. We saw that there are often several emotional layers to a problem. Hence, if the real problem is linked to pride, self-esteem or worthlessness, and the person is expressing anger or sadness, by offering our help to this "pseudo-problem", we are not helping by any means. At best, we will probably comfort the person by reinforcing his emotional state. Actually, because the sad person wants to be consoled and the angry person wants to be calmed down, when we intervene to try to help them, the message we are telling them is that it is alright to be sad or angry. But in reality, the sadness and anger are merely emotional reactions to something more and by helping them we prevent them from voluntarily seeking their deep emotions. Thus, the person listening must let the other person express everything that he feels before providing assistance. Otherwise it will slow down the process by which the real solution can be found. Only when all the emotions are expressed and truly felt will it be possible for the helper to assist.

The search for an immediate solution

Another common reflex in people who want to help others is to propose an immediate solution. In many people's minds there seems to be the equation 'problem → solution'. It is true that, to a degree, the goal of anyone wanting to help someone is to bring this other person to resolve his problems and difficulties. And it is also true that this is the way to proceed when it comes to solving cognitive, materialistic, and technical problems. However, when it comes to helping someone going through emotional problems, it is important to resist the temptation of wanting to propose an immediate solution. To solve other persons' problems is very good for self-esteem. But in reality, since we are removed from the other's problems, is it a simple thing to do to propose a customized solution, even with good intention. But if the problem that is exposed or the emotion that is expressed is not the real one, the proposed solution will not be the correct one either. The person experiencing the problem may elaborate yet deep down, this may not be the problem at all.

Let us take an example. A student explains to his teacher that he cannot find time to study and do his exercises. The teacher will assume that the student's lack of time to study is responsible for his bad grades and his first reaction might be to try to help the student by looking at how he could better manage his time, plan his agenda, or take advantage of his free time during the day. This is indeed what we would all try to do if we only relied on the student's first statement. But if we listen more astutely to the student we may discover that there is, for example, perhaps more time in a week that the student can use if we help to organize his agenda. But the real problem could be elsewhere. Let us imagine that this student has a very strong personality trait called "seeking novelty". In this case, it is likely that he may have a deep aversion to "monotonous" and less stimulating activities such as sitting down for hours to study. In addition, let us assume that he slowly developed a mental block toward studying because the frequent failures that he experienced have led him to doubt his intellectual abilities and to feel worthless. Therefore, in proposing solutions too quickly, as seen above, it will certainly not help him. Instead, it is by listening and paying close attention to this student's emotional and personal dynamics that we will be able to discover fundamental elements linked to his difficulties in school. And this understanding will allow us to explore with him a more appropriate way to manage his situation. But first, we must listen.

The analysis and the interpretation

Another way of intervening is to analyze and interpret what the person is telling us. Although this way corresponds to the stereotypical notion that we have of psychoanalysts who dissect each of our words and try to give them a meaning or an explanation. Very often we also have a tendency to project our interpretation on the person who has the problem in other words we start with a hypothesis and all the clues given by the other person serve to reinforce our interpretation. Confirming our interpretation can be rewarding but it generally leads to confusion.

It is, therefore, important to understand that the student who comes to us to share his problems tries to establish a trusting relationship with us. And he will be even more sensitive to everything that we will tell him and the interpretations that we will make of his situation. To this end, we must try to avoid, whenever possible, excessive interpretations and especially prematurely dwelling on long analyses of the problems expressed.

Sometimes attempts will be made to allow the student to clearly express what he is feeling. In this case, the teacher must be cautious and keep in mind that he can be wrong and, most importantly, that it is not for him to understand but for the student. If we are not careful, we will give the other person the impression that we understand the problem better than he does. And of course, this is not our aim; our goal is to help the other person. So, replies such as "I totally understand what you are going through", while they may be more gratifying to the person making them than to the person receiving them, are ineffectual when helping the student find a resolution to his emotional conflict.

The evaluation and the control

Evaluating a situation may well be more damaging than helpful in that it appears we may be judging an individual. What could be worse than being judged? Indian philosopher Krishnamurti said that the highest form of intelligence is to observe without judging. Evaluating creates exactly the opposite of higher intelligence. The one pretending to help usually makes comments, takes the liberty of sharing opinion on the experiences of others, judges others' behaviors, disapproves of others' choices, and underestimates others' reactions.

The majority of people, if not all, who seek help ask themselves if they are right, on the right track, if their action was correct, if they should have reacted differently, et cetera. This is perfectly understandable because if they had the feeling that their words, actions, and emotions were good, they would feel good and not seek help. But when there is doubt, hesitation, or insecurities with their own behaviors, then they do not feel good. Therefore, a teacher that takes the liberty to openly evaluate and judge a student does more harm than help. The student needs to feel that he is understood, accepted, loved, and not judged or condemned. You are not without knowing that guilt, doubt, and shame are the most widespread emotions and, more importantly, the most devastating. Evaluation and control are merely elements that add fuel to the flames. Carl Rogers explained that unconditional acceptance was one of the most important attributes of someone who provides assistance[129]. To accept someone in need is key because this is what the person seeks most. We all have, at one time or another, suffered or been sensitive to others' judgment of us. For this reason, it is critical that the person coming to us for help does not feel judged in any way but rather accepted as he is and be given the opportunity to openly express all that he is experiencing and feeling.

Furthermore, there is another element that can be detrimental to any situation; control. Many people have the habit of telling others how they should behave. It goes hand in hand with evaluation because if we judge others, why not tell them what to do and how they should behave? Those who judge are often equally skilled at telling others how to behave. In searching for a solution, control is only appropriate if it comes from the person seeking help. It is quite often true that the person who is helped will ask the teacher to evaluate him ("am I right?", "am I normal?", or "did I react appropriately?"). It is also true for the seeker to ask what he should do ("what do you recommend I do?", "tell me what I should do". And obviously he looks to himself for immediate solutions.

It goes without saying that the path to unconditional acceptance can only manifest if the teacher refrains from evaluating, judging, controlling, telling others what to do and giving others "good advice". In order to attain it, the teacher must disregard his own values as much as he can. We ought not to forget that judging is easier to do than understanding and accepting. Thus, an effort is required to achieve unconditional assistance and transform it into an art

The investigation

A popular technique with people trying to help is to adopt an aggressive questioning approach, like popular detectives Sherlock Holmes and Columbo. Of course, it is important to ask questions as long as they are pertinent and play a role in the assisting process. Questions must inform us on relevant elements and not simply casual curiosities. Hence, they must be limited in number and related to the situation so that it flows naturally.

---

129 Rogers, C.R. (1961).

Chapter 4

In addition, questions must be open-ended as they invite more elaboration and development. They must also be formulated in such a way that the person being helped will provide information instead of just answering questions. Open-ended questions relate to the how and why of things whereas close-ended ones can only be answered by a 'yes' or a 'no', or by a punctual element associated to a number, time, or space. When used too often they can put us in a position where one leads to another and ultimately we may find ourselves in a cul-de-sac.

Actually, the close-ended questions are like a trap in which we can easily fall especially if we use them frequently. "When did this happen?", "where did she go?", "how many times did this happen?", "did you get scared?", "was she upset? ", et cetera. All these questions will inevitably lead to brief and succinct answers such as; "last Wednesday", "at her dad's", "three times", "yes", and "no". For an inexperienced teacher, close-ended questions are definitely a trap because brief answers will result in him asking other close-ended questions seemingly without end and the teacher finds himself concentrating more on the next question rather than on how the student feels.

The table below summarizes the different listening attitudes and their consequences for the person seeking help.

Table 4.2
Different inefficient listening attitudes and their consequences

Listening attitude	Examples	Consequences on the person we are trying to help
Search for the immediate solution	Advising : "If I were you, I would review this subject" Giving solutions : "The best solution would be to ask your teacher for advice" Influencing the student's decision : "If I were you, I would go with them instead of doing nothing" Managing : "You should put your act together" Giving orders : "Go talk to him now" Threatening : "Solve this problem or else you will fail"	Remains unsatisfied with the solutions that he deems inefficient Feels misunderstood on what he is truly experiencing Feels trapped and obligated to accept the suggested solution that does not feel suited for his reality Loses confidence in himself and can become hostile toward the other person
Investigation	Investigating : "What did you do yesterday?" Questioning : "How long did you study for?" Interrogating : "Why did you write this?" Testing : "What will you do to avoid this in the future?"	Loses total concentration Loses sight of the real purpose of the conversation and the feelings he felt Can develop hostility against this investigation and implicit judgment Can become inhibited and back away
Compassionate support	Reassuring : "You'll see, things will work" Comforting : "Don't worry, things will get better soon you'll see" Approving without foundation : "Yes, you are right! The exam was very difficult" Compassionate : "I understand what you are saying... I had the same problem when I was a student" Supportive : "I am with you on this!"	Can trigger passivity and dependence Can feel condescension Can feel a despised patronizing attitude
Interpretation	Explaining : "You say this because you did not put out enough efforts"	Can lead to a lack of interest for the discussion, a phoney attitude to end it or make the

	Finding the causes and the intentions behind the other person's behavior : "You say this but the fact is that it's not the true reason!" Analyzing : "Your behavior may be the result of a personal problem" Diagnosing : "You lack discipline"	other person happy, or a change of subject You trigger a frustration for not being understood
Evaluation and control	Blaming : "It's your fault if things are that bad" Moralizing : "I told you that you had to work hard to succeed" Judging : "Your reaction was improper" Preaching : "A good student must study every day" Insulting : "You weren't too bright when dealing with this question" Humiliating : "You are incapable of succeeding in anything" To ridicule : "A child would do better" Approving (from a moral standpoint) : "Finally, you do what you should be doing!" Complimenting (while judging) : "Usually you have a better judgment"	Can undermine his self-esteem and self-confidence Can trigger an inhibiting behavior Can trigger internal and external rebellion Can undermine motivation Can trigger guilt, rebellion, anguish, or the emotion of feeling down

The empathetic listening

Here is an extraordinary story with a disconcerting simplicity reported by Marshall B. Rosenberg[130]. It is about a little schoolgirl who was feeling down while waiting for the principal. As soon as she saw the little girl, the principal sat down next to her and asked her what was wrong.

Miss Anderson, she said, did you ever spend an entire week where all your actions were doing wrong to people around you when, in fact, all you were trying to do is help? Yes, she replied. I understand what you mean. So, the little schoolgirl started telling her story of what had happened that week. But the principal, who still had her coat on and who was in a rush because she had a meeting, asked little Jessica : "what can I do for you?" The little girl got closer

130 Rosenberg, M. B. (1999).

and, with a hand on the principal's shoulder, looked at her right in the eye and said : "Miss Anderson, I am not asking you to do anything for me. I am simply asking you to listen to me."

Here is a beautiful lesson. As Carl Rogers explains, empathetic listening "allows us to perceive our universe in a different light and move forward."

Let us examine how we can practice empathetic listening.

The reformulation

It is highly probable that most of you are familiar with the "reformulation" listening technique. However, knowing it does not necessarily mean that you put it into practice and, much less, that you have mastered it. Even so, reformulating is one of the most significant ways of listening.

The technique of reformulation consists of repeating in our own terms what the person talking to us has said as accurately as possible. At first, many people may be uncomfortable with this method because they have the feeling that they are like parrots repeating what the other person said without thinking. Yet rest assured that even if you feel this way at first, you soon are amazed at how efficient it is and the results it can bring.

To use an analogy, we can compare reformulation to jumping on a trampoline. Each rebound takes us higher than the previous bounce. And this is what happens when we reformulate the sentences of the person speaking to us. He gives us a sentence, we reformulate it, he confirms what we said and adds other elements, and then we reformulate again, and so on. Thus, the power of this technique is threefold. First, our interlocutor feels that he is being listened to and understood because to apply this technique, you must acknowledge what the other is saying. Someone who is distracted cannot proceed with reformulation. Second, our interlocutor has no other choice than to go a little deeper because you have confirmed that you understood what he said. And thirdly, the person speaking may learn things about himself because from time to time he will say things without realizing it and only when he hears your reformulation will he realize what he said. Only at this stage will he begin to understand what he expressed.

Very few people are accustomed to being listened to when they speak and many people speak without being fully aware of what they say. This is why we often become lost in a jumble, or swim in a sea of useless babble. Not only do people listen very little to what the other person says, but they also pay too much attention to what they are going to say.

Thus, reformulation is to a teacher what a hammer is to a carpenter, an indispensable tool. It can take on several forms :

> ➤ It can consist of simply repeating exactly what the other person said. This is the safest way as it leaves no room for interpretations;

- It can consist of "reformulating" using other words, synonyms, or analogies;
- It can consist of simply repeating the few last words of the sentence. For instance, the person says : "the other day, my girlfriend and I went to visit her mom". You can reformulate by saying : "...to visit her mom!". In this case, the other person has no other choice than to follow : "...yes! It was her birthday and my girlfriend finds it important to go visit her mom on this occasion."
- It can also be stated with a question : "So you went to visit your girlfriend's mom because it's important for her, is this right?" In this case, the question becomes a reformulation because it takes the main elements of the other person's statement and turns it into a question. The interlocutor will then follow the same way he would if the reformulation were an affirmation.

The reflection

The 'reflection' listening method consists of essentially reflecting to the other person his feelings and emotions. Its role is to highlight the emotional statements of the other person. In this situation, there is a good chance that he will add more emotional character to his statements. This is, in fact, the goal of the person who practices empathetic listening, to have the interlocutor switch from statements of facts and behaviors to statements of feelings and emotions in order to gear the discussion toward deeper levels of expression and understanding. In this way, by exploring his feelings and emotions, the student will develop his awareness. The same methods as those used for reformulation can be used :

- Reformulating the aspects of the interlocutor's statement that have to do with feelings and emotions : "when my girlfriend told me that she was going to visit her mom, I did not like it because I don't like the atmosphere over there". Reflection : "...you do not like the atmosphere at your in-laws…"
- It can consist of using other words than those mentioned by the interlocutor to reflect his feelings : "...you felt discomfort with the thought of visiting your girlfriend's mom"
- We can also question the emotion : "... how does the atmosphere at your in-laws affect you?"

The focalization

The focalization listening method involves concentrating specifically on an emotional element brought about by the interlocutor. In other words, we can decide on developing an aspect in the discussion that we feel is pertinent and invite the other person to elaborate further. Generally speaking, focalization will touch on feelings and emotions. Therefore, the person listening will guide the other person toward these elements and will ask him to expand, asking for more details and additional explanations. Thus, he will examine more closely an emotional aspect that he perceived and deemed important. As opposed to investigation, focalization is more pertinent because it directly addresses the other person's problem and what he feels. As we know, it is central to thoroughly explore the emotions that the interlocutor feels and focalization is a great tool that will allow this kind of exploration. Unfortunately, by concentrating on one aspect of the problem, it may remove the attention from the global problem. This is why it becomes important for you to make links that will help the other person understand the relationship that exists between the emotional dimensions that you address and his problem as a whole. Thus, focalization implies making a short summary of the problem by tying together the statements made. This will result in the student being able to understand the link between what he is experiencing, doing, and feeling.

The confrontation

By far, confrontation is the most difficult listening technique because it forces the student to call into question certain aspects of his problem and become more self-aware. Therefore, the goal of confrontation is to 'force' the interlocutor to go explore deeper into the problem. Sometimes he will acknowledge a few absurdities and inconsistencies in his statements and he will have to question himself and move on to something else.

Confrontation is an art and has nothing to do with creating a hostile environment. Nor is the one who confronts there to create discord or resistance. Instead, this art presents itself in style and diplomacy and must be perfectly timed. In order to confront you must be sure to have many elements at your disposal otherwise the other person may slip away, justify himself and withdraw. Moreover, this technique must rest on very precise elements so that the student knows exactly what is at stake. Without intimidating, confrontation is a shock that has an impact on consciousness by 'forcing' the other person to face some feelings that he is trying to avoid or ignore. In any case, this method is effective and leads to something new. It can help bring out new and unexpressed aspects that had been previously hidden or perhaps enhance the meaninglessness of what has been expressed.

Here is an example of a conversation between a teacher and a student :

Teacher :	So Peter, what can I do for you?
Peter :	I'm not sure what I'm doing here. I feel like dropping out.
Teacher :	You feel like giving up your educational? [reformulation]
Peter :	Actually, it's the people who get on my nerves. They're all so stupid and narrow-minded.
Teacher :	You don't feel good in their presence... [reflection]
Peter :	No. There are cliques everywhere in this school...
Teacher :	And you find it difficult to communicate with them... [reflection]
Peter :	How do you expect to communicate with people who are narrow-minded and who think of themselves as the center of the world?
Teacher :	Is this the reason why you are always alone when I see you in the cafeteria? [confrontation]
Peter :	long silence ... his eyes are becoming watery ... shrugging his shoulders.

Teacher :	You feel alone in this school and this is why you want to leave [confrontation]
Peter :	Yes, maybe. It's not easy to be rejected by everybody.
Teacher :	You feel rejected by others [reflection]
Peter :	Yes. I cannot make friends here. I feel so different from everyone else in this school.
Teacher :	You would like to have more friends [reflection]
Peter :	Of course! Isn't this normal?
Teacher :	Because there are some people with whom you would like to make friends? [confrontation]
Peter :	Yes. There are some who are interesting after all.
Teacher :	But you don't find it easy to go talk to them and become friends with them. [reflection]
Peter :	No. I've always been too shy to talk to other people.

In the example above, Peter starts by expressing anger toward school and all the other students and wants to drop out. A reformulating and a few reflective statements from the teacher have helped to bring out Peter's difficulty with communication. But it truly is the two confrontational statements "Is this the reason why you are always alone when I see you at the cafeteria?" and "You feel alone in this school and this is why you want to leave," that have highlighted Peter's feeling of being rejected and isolated. Then, the reflective statements further helped Peter to express a deep desire to have friends. With that came a new confrontation, "Because there are some people with whom you would like to be friends with?" which 'forced' Peter to admit that there were, after all, a few people he would like to befriend. Finally, the reflection has led him to express his shyness and difficulty communicating.

Each time that the confrontation approach is used, it forces the interlocutor to reach a new emotional depth; the feeling of rejection, shyness, et cetera. At this point, the teacher will be able to help the student overcome his shyness. It is interesting to realize that if the teacher would have allowed himself to be 'trapped' by the first statements, he would have tried to convince Peter to stay in school because it is important for his success and future and would have been completely off track.

Let us not forget that the person being helped will only change parameters of his story if he understands full well what goes on inside of him. It is not just about identifying the problem but also understanding the mechanisms involved. Thus, the confrontational approach creates a shock in the person's consciousness and leads to something new. It is, no doubt, a powerful tool that should be used cautiously, carefully employed only when necessary.

The one who uses this technique must be prepared to understand what follows. As mentioned earlier in the case of focalization, confrontation leads to a better understanding thus, the role of the teacher is to stitch together the fragmented elements expressed by the student. And in order to do so, he must focus his attention to what is being expressed and remember the important aspects of the problem without losing sight of the deeper issue. In turn, the student who moves through the different layers of his problem may not necessarily be able to piece everything together. Thus, from time to time the helper will have to give an overview of the situation.

The synthesis

The synthesis summarizes the essential elements of the problem and brings them together. It draws a general overview of the situation, which is then presented to the student, allowing him to have a more clear and global vision of the situation. The consequence of this listening method is that it takes the person being helped to new paths and depths pointing to a possible solution to the problem.

Teacher : So Peter, your struggle to communicate with others makes you want to drop out of school. This is also the reason why you find them stupid and narrow-minded. But actually, what you say is that there are some people who are interesting in school but you are too shy to talk to them. As a result, you isolate yourself even more. Is this correct? [synthesis]

Peter : Yes! This is it in a nutshell. I would so very much like to be comfortable enough to talk to them but I'm always afraid to bother them or be judged by them. Sometimes, I imagine myself talking to them and two minutes later I become speechless. I feel paralysed.

Exercise 4.3
Listening

Instructions : Go back to the exercise 4.2 and try to identify the listening method you have used in the proposed examples. Did you have a tendency to propose immediate solutions or to offer compassionate support or to evaluate? Or perhaps you opted for the empathetic listening approach.

For each statement, try to reply using the empathetic listening approach.

Michael tells you, after receiving a bad score on his exam : "I cannot believe this! I studied like a mad man for this test. I cannot understand why I got this score" [131].
Reply :

Mary tells you, after you ask her why she still has not returned her homework: "I tried to do it several times but I don't understand what I need to do. The instructions are not clear."
Reply :

You cross Paul in the hallway and he does not seem too happy. You ask : "is everything Okays Paul?" Well... I just walked out of a French exam with Brown. He really is vicious with his questions. Everybody feel that they flunked his exam. In fact, the teacher warned us that the majority of students would fail. It's appalling! [132]
Reply :

Carol pays you a visit at your office : "I would like to have more time before returning my homework. I will have three exams next week and will not be able to do it. On top of it, I must go to my cousin's wedding [133]."
Reply :

---

131 Example of an empathetic reply : "you are surprised to have received such a bad score on your exam." We have identified the 'surprise' at the beginning of the sentence "I cannot believe this!", which implies an emotion.
132 Example of an empathetic reply : "you are upset at your teacher." We have identified the emotion of anger by relying on Paul's expression "he really is vicious". We could have also emphasized the disgust that he expressed when he said "it's appalling."
133 Example of an empathetic reply : "you're afraid that you won't have time to do everything." We have identified the emotion of fear relying on the fact that Carol refers to the many things she needs to do soon.

Managing emotions

How to help the student manage his emotions?

After helping the student identify, express, and understand his emotions, we can examine how we can help him manage them. In chapter 3, we covered different facets of emotional management. We have also identified the management of primary and secondary emotions as well as the management of background emotions. Thus, it is important to understand that the former is not managed the same way as the latter. Indeed, primary and secondary emotions emerge very rapidly and have an immediate and excessive impact on attention, perception, concentration, and memorization. In terms of background emotions, they fluctuate in a more subtle manner over time and surge with less intensity, but they have an equally negative impact. In other words, they will interfere considerably with the cognitive processes and consequently affect the learning process.

The management of primary emotions

Below are the five components of emotions, as described in more detail in chapter 3 :

- ➢ nonverbal expressions;
- ➢ physiological reactions;
- ➢ behavioral reactions;
- ➢ cognitions;
- ➢ emotional feelings.

In chapter 3, we have also mentioned that the management of emotions went through each of these components. Thus, when it is time to manage our own emotions we can touch on each of these components because they are within us and it is possible to exert control over them. However, when it comes to helping someone else manage their emotions, we have less control on these components. Even so, we can still play a huge role more than we realize. Let us examine a few examples of actions or activities that we can implement to help students manage emotions that are harmful to the learning process.

Managing nonverbal expressions as well as physiological and behavioral reactions

Because they have a strong connection, we will treat these three components simultaneously.

Firstly, we should try to detect the students' emotions when you teach a class, when they are working on an exercise, or when they are in a study or exam session. In the previous pages, we have amply discussed the detection of others' emotions. As we know, empathy and vigilance toward nonverbal signals are indispensable in order to perceive the students' emotions when they surface. Hence, one of the best times to detect nonverbal signals is when the class subject is dull and unenthusiastic. In this case, nonverbal signals become more numerous and more explicit; body posture, facial expressions of frustration and disgust, jerky movements, et cetera. Thus, the teacher who can perceive these signs can intervene quickly and act immediately. An example could be to interrupt the exercise or the class and ask all the students to stand up and start moving, stretching, breathing deeply, et cetera. The important point here is to have them engage their entire body. Table 4.3 presents different exercises or scenarios that are easy to put in place and that try to interrupt the emotional rhythm caused by certain teaching or learning situations.

Table 4.3
Exercises and scenarios that try to modify students' nonverbal expressions as well as physiological and behavioral reactions

Name of the exercise	Description	Effect of the exercise
Broadening the field of perception[134]	Broadening of the field of vision: Invite students to put both hands in front of their eyes (index pointing to the ceiling), ~12 inches away. Then invite them to slowly move their hands sideways in order to broaden their peripheral vision as much as possible. Broadening of other senses : Invite students to close their eyes and try to perceive, from their environment, the most sounds; the most smells; the most tastes they have in their mouths; the most sensations from the clothes on their skin including rings, watches, the sensations of the chair on their back and buttocks, et cetera.	When we are emotional and tensed, it has been shown that our perceptual field shrinks. And carrying out this broadening exercise creates relaxation, allows us to better perceive the possibilities that are offered to us and, most of all, allows us to stand back and see the big picture.
Breathing	Invite students to sit comfortably on their chair and take a few very deep breaths (inhales and exhales) without creating any tension. This breathing must also be done using the abdomen (belly) and	Since it is possible to reproduce a negative emotional state by recreating its corresponding breathing pattern, it is also possible to do so for a positive emotion. Thus, the goal of this exercise

---

134 We have special devices designed to help you carry out this type of exercise. For more information, please go to www.emotionalpedagogy.com

	not the shoulders.	is to decrease the physiological response (autonomous nervous system and stress hormones) brought about by negative emotions.
Draining	Invite students to stand and close their eyes. Then, after taking three deep breaths, invite them to let their head slowly lean forward. In a fluid and constant motion, the upper body follows the movement from the top to the bottom, until the person is completely inclined, head down and arms on each side. Hold a few seconds and then, go back to an upright position by slowly unfolding the spine.	Negative emotions always come with a significant production of harmful chemical substances that travel all over our body and, more specifically, get stuffed in our brain. Thus, the goal of this exercise is to drain the brain by bringing fresh blood to it. The downward inclination creates hyperaemia (an engorgement of blood in the brain) and the recovery to an upright position allows the draining to take place. This exercise brings a sensation of clarity to our thoughts and ideas.
Stretching	Invite students to stand and stretch as much as they can – as if they wanted to grab the stars with their hands. Then have them take a seat and stretch their legs forward curling their toes up toward them.	In stressful situations, our muscles have a tendency to tense up and tighten while this exercise will have the opposite effect.
Energetic contact	All the students stand up in line and form a huge circle. Then, each one will gently massage the shoulders of the person in front of them. After a while, everyone turns around and massage the person that was behind them.	Teaching students to touch each other with respect and without a sexual connotation will develop empathy, friendship between them and, of course, will relax them and increase their energy.
Create a positive thought	Everyone will stand up on their desk with their arms up and shout, as loud as they can : "I am the queen (or king) of the world"	This will help students to improve their self-esteem and create new positive connections in their brain.
Upside down world	In groups of 2, back-to-back and 3 feet apart, have the	We know that emotions modify our perceptions of

Chapter 4

| | students bend over to the floor and throw a ball to each other using their hands and feet. After a few seconds, they will feel like they are on the ceiling and that everything is upside down. | events. Hence, to change our body postures and our ways of looking at the world can help to understand things differently. |
| Smiling | Have your students put a pencil between their teeth as if they were smiling. Then, they do a little exercise called jumping jack. | Some studies showed that the facial and corporal expression of an emotion is conducive of intensifying the emotional feeling attached to it. |

In addition to exercises proposed in table 4.3, you can easily imagine a large number of short exercises that contribute to the students' well-being. The idea is to show students how to directly intervene in situations that can trigger negative emotions. Hence, this is a pro-active approach. Table 4.4 summarizes the 9-step method proposed by D'Zurilla[135].

---

135 See Lazarus, R. S. (1991).

Table 4.4
The 9-step technique of resolving emotional problems

Step	Description	Example
1	Evaluate the situation that generates an emotion and set a tangible goal	A student is annoyed by the fact that his project partner is not doing anything. The first step is to define the problem precisely and determine what the student plans on doing
2	Objectively evaluate the inadequate way you deal with the problems in your life	The student must examine how he usually reacts to his partner's behavior and why his reactions are inefficient
3	Examine what role your emotions play in resolving your problem	The student notices that such-and-such behavior from his partner inevitably irritates him. Therefore, he admits that this emotional reaction will prevent him from solving the problem and that anger is not an option as it will make things worse
4	Examine a precise example where the emotional problem comes up and analyze the exact circumstances that cause it to surface	The student must ask himself if he reacts emotionally to the fact that his partner procrastinates until the moment he does the work himself. He must then examine precisely what is happening under those circumstances and why he is reacting as he does
5	To set a realistic goal that is directly related to this situation	His goal could be to no longer become upset because it is counterproductive and negatively affects his humor
6	List as many solutions to the situation as possible	The student can decide not to do his partner's work and, seeing his partner's nonchalance, explain to him calmly that this is how things will be from now on. He can also decide to take a few minutes with his partner and ask him to be more disciplined. Or he can also decide to let things drag until his partner realizes himself that nothing is being done and that they might soon face a problem
7	Take each of these solutions and assess which one is the most satisfactory and efficient at solving the situation	The student chooses to take a few minutes with his partner to ask him to be more disciplined

8	Apply the solution that you chose and assess its efficiency	After discussing things clearly with his partner, the student waits for a few days and sees what happens
9	Depending on the results, if they are not satisfactory, opt for another solution and go back to step 8	If the proposed solution does not bear any fruits, try another option

Managing our cognitions

As we all know, cognitions often come with most emotions. When an emotion is felt during a situation, we generally all have an internal monologue-taking place. And because of this, the teacher has practically no control over what a student thinks when he reacts emotionally. Yet, he has the ability to listen and help the student express what he is feeling but no power to modify his thoughts. In other words, it is very difficult to imagine what someone is thinking and instill different thoughts. Worst yet, wanting to modify the other person's thoughts will result in reinforcing his existing thoughts and convince him that he is right. It is, therefore, important for the student to acknowledge by himself that his negative thoughts can have an impact on his well-being. Once again, first and foremost, the one who wants to help must listen to the other person without rushing to find an immediate solution and without interpreting or judging. The more a teacher guides his student toward the expression of his emotions and needs, the more he will allow him to understand why he reacts a certain way. This will then make him realize that his emotions and needs go hand in hand. In this he will be able to identify negative and harmful emotions. Table 4.5 shows the main thoughts that are associated with and maintain negative emotions.

Table 4.5
Types of negative thoughts

Types of thoughts	Examples
Extreme generalizations	John struggles with his math exercises. He tells himself : "I absolutely understand nothing in math... I've always been hopeless with calculations... I've never been good at it... ".
Catastrophic predictions	After failing an exam, Karen tells herself : "I'm going to fail my entire year and I'll never be able to attend any universities with such scores..."
Excuses (ex causa = external causes)	Mary got a bad score on her exam : "it's the teacher's fault if things are going so bad... his exams are always written to make everyone fail..."
Self-demeaning thoughts	David blames himself for the slightest mistake : "I'm so hopeless and worthless... everyone else understands except me..."

Managing emotions

Exercise 4.4
Identifying our own negative thoughts

Instruction 1 : Invite a student to identify certain situations that make him react emotionally. To help him, use the table below.

Situation category	Description of the situation	Emotions felt	Intensity of the emotion
Time	----------------- ----------------- ----------------- ----------------- ----------------- -----------------	--------------- --------------- --------------- --------------- --------------- ---------------	1 2 3 4 5 1 2 3 4 5 1 2 3 4 5 1 2 3 4 5 1 2 3 4 5 1 2 3 4 5
Class subject (Spanish, math, physics, et cetera.)	----------------- ----------------- ----------------- ----------------- ----------------- -----------------	--------------- --------------- --------------- --------------- --------------- ---------------	1 2 3 4 5 1 2 3 4 5 1 2 3 4 5 1 2 3 4 5 1 2 3 4 5 1 2 3 4 5
Teaching activity (exercise, skilful exposé, way of explaining, et cetera.)	----------------- ----------------- ----------------- ----------------- ----------------- -----------------	--------------- --------------- --------------- --------------- --------------- ---------------	1 2 3 4 5 1 2 3 4 5 1 2 3 4 5 1 2 3 4 5 1 2 3 4 5 1 2 3 4 5
Evaluations (exams, assignments, et cetera.)	----------------- ----------------- ----------------- ----------------- ----------------- -----------------	--------------- --------------- --------------- --------------- --------------- ---------------	1 2 3 4 5 1 2 3 4 5 1 2 3 4 5 1 2 3 4 5 1 2 3 4 5 1 2 3 4 5
Relationships (team work, other students disturbing, interpersonal conflicts, et cetera.)	----------------- ----------------- ----------------- ----------------- ----------------- -----------------	--------------- --------------- --------------- --------------- --------------- ---------------	1 2 3 4 5 1 2 3 4 5 1 2 3 4 5 1 2 3 4 5 1 2 3 4 5 1 2 3 4 5

Instruction 2 : Once the situations have been identified, invite the student to describe the thoughts he has regarding these situations and specify the type of thinking these situations belong to. (see table 4.5).

Description of a situation in relation to time :

Description of the thoughts in relation to the situation :

Which type of thinking do these thoughts belong to (Extreme generalizations, catastrophic predictions, excuses, self-demeaning thoughts):

Managing emotions

Once these thoughts are identified, the teacher will then be able to help the student manage them. Indeed, without being able to change them for him, he will be able to help the student do it on his own.

In fact, cognitive psychologists propose a 3-step process to repress irrational and catastrophic thoughts that come along with negative thoughts. Table 4.6 summarizes this method :

Table 4.6
Technique used to repress negative thoughts

Step	Description	Example
1	When facing an emotional situation, we must take a few moments to examine our thoughts and beliefs with regard to the situation	The student who feels anxiety when taking an exam can foster many irrational thoughts such as : "It's horrible, I'm going blank", "I'm damned; I'm going to flunk my semester", "I knew I was hopeless; everything I do is always awful", "I'm too hyperactive", "my heart is going to explode if it keeps on beating like this", et cetera. The student acknowledges these irrational and catastrophic thoughts and recognizes the role they play in the emotional process
2	After acknowledging these negative thoughts, replace them with positive and constructive thoughts	The student can repeat these positive thoughts in his head many times : "relax, you know the class subject, it will come back to you", "It's not because you cannot pass this test that your life is over; you will do better next time", "answer the questions one by one and then evaluate", "take a deep breath and let go of your tension", et cetera.
3	Reward yourself by congratulating yourself mentally for changing your thought processes and beliefs	The student then tells himself : "Good! Now you see how good it feels when you are positive", "keep on following this path, everything is fine", et cetera.

Chapter 4

Instruction 3 : After identifying negative thoughts and which thinking category they belong to, invite the student to understand the impact that they have on his emotional state and to replace them with more rational and realistic ones.

Describe how these thoughts can affect your emotional state :

List more positive and constructive thoughts that are related to the experienced situation :

Managing our needs

Another course of action consists of helping students manage their irrational needs. Table 4.7 summarizes the main irrational needs.

Table 4.7
Irrational needs

Irrational needs
To be right
To control
To be loved
To be appreciated
To be approved of
To be perfect
To be acknowledged
To be useful
To possess
Power
To feel free
Security
To feel valued

To help the student manage his needs, the teacher must succeed in highlighting them. Empathetic listening is a good way to achieve this goal. In addition, reflection and focalization will contribute enormously in helping the student isolate the irrational needs that are related to the emotions he is feeling. Then, confrontation will ensure that the student will put them in perspective. More specifically, the confrontation of the needs with the true facts can lead the person expressing these needs to make them more relative to the situation and not view them as definitive results. For instance, the student who is obsessed with perfection might be disappointed to get a score of 95 percent because he will focus on the few wrong answers he had rather than the many good ones. The same goes for the student who has an excessive need to be loved, to be approved of, or to control. As we saw in chapter 3, it is unrealistic to believe that we can satisfy all of these needs. In other words, it is highly unlikely that we can be loved by all people, be perfect, or control everybody. This is why we must learn how to manage these needs because they can cause so much harm. We cannot simply tell people to detach themselves from their irrational and illusive needs but to help them become aware of these needs and illuminate them. And before prematurely confronting the student to the irrationality of his needs, it is important to help him to acknowledge that they exist and that they can create a lot of damage if he continues to harbor them. To do so, we propose a simple and efficient technique for helping your students feel better.

The APIE[*] method consists of asking four questions to the person so that he can quickly identify his emotions and needs and become aware of their negative impact (see table 4.8)[**].

Table 4.8
The four steps of the APIE[136] method

Step	Example	Objective
The Affect	"How do you feel about this situation?"	Invites the student to identify and express his emotions
The Predominantly difficult	"What do you find the most difficult in this situation?"	Allows the student to pinpoint the fundamental emotion and express what it all means to him
The Irrational need	"If you could, what would you change in this situation?"	By placing the student in the core of the question, his response will help you identify his irrational need
The Emergence	"If I understand what you are saying, you need…"	By reformulating the answer to the previous question to help him describe his irrational need, the student acknowledges this need and, thus, becomes able to deal with it in a more rational way

To begin with, you must have a clear idea of the situation. It is not necessary to delve into details but it is important to have a general idea of what is going on with the student. To do so, you must allow the student to freely express himself for a few minutes without interrupting. David Servan-Schreiber suggests letting the person express himself for no more than approximately three minutes otherwise we run the risk of overwhelming ourselves with unneeded and superfluous details[137]. In fact, the most important are not the facts but rather the emotions. Therefore, getting to the first question is essential.

A The **A**ffect. The first question tries to explore the person's affect (the conscious subjective aspect of his feeling(s) or emotion(s)) in order for him to identify and express how he feels in the situation. After listening to him relates his situation, you simply ask him : "how do you feel about this situation?" or "what emotion did you feel?". It is important for the person to name the emotion(s) that he felt and, specifically in this instance, that you adopt

---

* The APEI method is taught at the Acadamy of Pleasurology and Emotional Intelligence (APEI) (see www.apie.ca) and at the Emotional Pedagogy Institute (see www.emotionalpedagogy.com).
** Because the APIE method was developed in French and the English translation of the acronym becomes APEI. But here, we will keep the French acronym as the sequence is very important.
136 The APEI method is inspired by the BATHE method developed by Joseph Lieberman and Marian Stuart. See : Lieberman, J.A., Stuard, M.R. (1999).
137 Servan-Schreiber, D. (2004).

empathetic listening. By using the reflection listening method described earlier in this chapter you can help the person further clarify his emotions. Then comes the second question.

P The **P**redominantly difficult. The second question takes us a little deeper in the emotional expression. This question is : "what do you find the most difficult in this situation?", or "what do you find the most troubling?", or "what do you find the most disturbing in all of this?". If you deem it necessary, this question can also be preceded by a short summary of what the person described and expressed to you up until that point. This question is powerful because it allows the person expressing himself to quickly pinpoint the emotion that is at the heart of his problem. It is a way to focus on the main emotion yet at the same time, it is possible that the person may have an intense emotional reaction in which case all you have to do is welcome it. You must also remind yourself that this is a very important phase in the process of the person's understanding of himself. And then, the third question.

I The **I**rrational need. The third question tries to highlight the person's need(s). It is worded in a way that compels the person to give a somewhat illogical answer. So the question should look like this : "if you could, what would you change in this situation?" or, if it is about someone else's behavior "how would you like this person to behave toward you?". Let us imagine this scenario; a student is stressed because the end of the semester is near and he still has a lot of work finishing his projects and studying for his finals. Imagine that he told you about this work overload that overwhelms him and the stress that affects him (Affect). When you ask him what he finds the most difficult, he replies that he is afraid to fail and to disappoint his parents, especially his father who expects a lot from him. Then when you ask him what he would change in the situation, if he could change something (irrational need), his reply is that he would love to be more intelligent or be as good as his brother Marc is. This reply suggests a need to be perfect. On the other hand, if he replied that he would love for his father to understand that he is trying his best, then this would suggest a need to be recognized and loved. This is when the door to the last step opens up.

E The **E**mergence. This is the ultimate step of the entire process. It allows the person who is gripped by an irrational and illusory need which is detrimental to his health to move on to something else. The emergence includes two phases. The first phase consists of reformulating the person's answer to the previous question in a way that expresses a need. For instance, when the student tells you that he would love to be more intelligent or be as good as his brother Marc, you can reformulate his reply like this; "if I understand what you are saying, you would love to be perfect." Conversely, if the student says that he would love for his father to understand that he is trying his best, you could say : "you would love for your dad to recognize all your efforts" or "you would love for your dad to appreciate you more." At this point of the discussion, this reformulation is confronting and is shocking to the other person. In other words, he is starting to feel something different, something that goes beyond what he said. Let us not forget that the same logic applies not only when it comes to helping someone recover his serenity but also to help this person learn. The goal really is to get him to feel. And even if our reason tells us that our needs are irrational this does not mean at all that we can solve them simply. If the student in our example logically understands the irrational aspect of his need to be perfect or approved, he has still not reached the idea that he will feel better afterwards. It is not enough that a person understands that he has a problem and what triggered it. In order to solve it, he must feel something that is linked to the problem. Thus, the shock created by a clear reformulation of his needs will enable him to feel something significant and at the same time will allow him to act in a way that will empower him and improve his well-being. For example, if the student comes to recognize that he always tries to be perfect and does not accept making mistakes, he will be able to downplay his needs and even detach himself from them. The second phase of the emergence consists of asking the person what would be the best thing to do for him to feel better. The awareness of his needs and how they relate to his negative emotions from the situation will not miraculously solve everything but will eventually take the person to the path of wellness. Thus, the empathy and the compassion that you will show will help this person feel better and sense your support as well.

Let us illustrate once more the APIE method using an example of a dialog between a teacher and a student. You will see there may be intermediate questions or interventions necessary to clarify certain points with the person[*].

It involves Nadia who has been studying computer science for almost two years.

Nadia :	I am sick of computer science. I feel like quitting everything.
Teacher :	Why do you say that?
Nadia :	Because I will never go anywhere with that discipline. My neighbor studied in this field and now he is unemployed. On top of it, the College's equipment is obsolete. We are learning using equipments that will not even exist when I'll graduate.
Teacher :	Are you re-evaluating your career path? (reflection)
Nadia :	Yes, that's it! I am completely re-evaluating my career path because computer science is not for me.
Teacher :	How do you feel in this re-evaluation process? (Affect)
Nadia :	I don't feel good because if I quit this field, I'm not sure what I'm going to do. I don't want to end up like some of my friends, i.e., without work and looking for jobs here and there.
Teacher :	What do you find the most difficult with respect to how you currently feel? (The predominantly difficult)
Nadia :	What I find the most difficult... (silence) ... I don't know. I think that if I give up, I'll feel like I'm worthless. I can see myself quitting one more time. Last year, I quit the swimming team and before that, it was my guitar class. I can never succeed in anything.

* Specialized seminars on the APEI method are taught at the Academy of Pleasurology and Emotional Intelligence (See www.apie.ca) and at the Emotional Pedagogy Institute (see www.emotionalpedagogy.com).

Managing emotions

Teacher :	And if you could change something in your situation, what would that be? (The irrational need)
Nadia :	I would like to achieve something one day, succeed in a goal that I set for myself.
Teacher :	You would like to prove to yourself that you can succeed in something (First phase of the emergence; confrontation by wording the need to feel worthy).
Nadia :	(a tear rolls down her cheek). Yes. I've never done anything good in my life. Things just don't go the way I want. I just feel like giving up.
Teacher :	What would help you not to give up this time, and go all the way through? (Second phase of the emergence; what to do to feel better).
Nadia :	(long silence) ... stop putting so much pressure on myself.
Teacher :	What do you mean?
Nadia :	Well, when I see that I don't have the best grades or I encounter difficulties, it's as if everything was crumbling and I started doubting myself. When I was younger, I always wanted to be number one in everything (awareness of the need to be perfect). I was competing against everyone and if I did not end up the winner, I would get really angry and would want to stop before the game is over.
Teacher :	A little bit like you are doing now with your computer science classes...
Nadia :	Yes. That's it! When things are not as easy as I would want them to be, I just want to give up.
Teacher :	Do you think that you can put less pressure on yourself? (going back to the second step of the emergence).
Nadia :	Yes. I think I can. All I need is to accept the fact that things don't always exactly go the way we want and if they don't, it doesn't mean that everything has to end.

In chapter 6, we will expound more on these notions when we address the personality profiles. We will see how to deal with these needs in relation to the person's profile, and will also examine some tips that will help consider the students' needs according to their personality.

Managing our emotional feelings and background emotions

As discussed in chapter 3, the management of background emotions is triggered by the stimulation of positive emotional states. We have seen that negative emotions were associated with an increased activity of the right prefrontal cortex, while positive emotions were lateralized in the left prefrontal cortex. We have also mentioned that when the person feels positive emotions, the activity of the left prefrontal lobes triggers the inhibition of the amygdala, the structure in the brain responsible for the negative emotions.

The management of background emotions is peculiar. Studies have shown that the strong desire to control an emotion could have an opposite effect. Indeed, any attempt to suppress "exciting thoughts" could result in an increased electrodermal response, which translates to an emotional activation. Similar results were observed on subjects who were shown repulsive images and who had to inhibit their expressions of disgust at the same time. These subjects showed that the stifling of negative emotions was associated with an increase in the activation of the amygdala. In short, these data show that we should not make an effort to suppress our emotions. Otherwise, when the "willingness" to suppress an emotion is too strong, it can trigger other emotions. Thus, emotional management must come naturally and without efforts. These results are consistent with the fact that forcing ourselves to inhibit certain negative emotions is an unpleasant feeling that activates our amygdala.

It becomes evident that the best way to manage our negative emotions is to arouse positive ones. As discussed in chapter 3, scientific data support the idea that positive emotions are the best tools to help manage negative emotions. Let us recall the three most important discoveries :

Paul Ekman and Richard Davidson have shown that by simply smiling we could trigger an activation of the left prefrontal cortex[138]. Richard Davidson, et al., have shown that meditation could activate the left prefrontal cortex[139]. Relaxation and meditation have shown their positive effects on the learning process[140].

This data brings us back to two notions :
1. Positive emotions and pleasure have an extraordinary potential; not only do they instill a sense of well-being, but they also help us react appropriately when facing different situations in our lives. Thus, we must try to stimulate the students' pleasure feelings in order to help them better understand;
2. Meditation, relaxation, and yoga all have a positive impact on the students' emotional state and consequently on their ability to learn. Therefore, we must try to include these practices in their classrooms in order to help them relax and have a positive attitude. This topic will be addressed in greater detail in chapter 6.

Managing background emotions through pleasure
We have identified four categories of pleasure[141] :
➤ Physiopleasure
➤ Sociopleasure
➤ Psychopleasure
➤ Ideopleasure

Let us describe them one by one.

1. Physiopleasure deals with the pleasure of the senses (taste, smell, sound, sight, and touch), the pleasure of sensuality (eating, drinking, caressing, smelling a perfume, and listening to music), and the pleasure of sexuality. The school environment should, therefore, trigger as much physiopleasure as possible. But unfortunately, this is not the case. Most classrooms do not have this notion in

---

138 Ekman, P. & Davidson, R.J. (1993).
139 Davidson, R. J., Kabat-Zinn, J., Schumacher, J., Rosenkrantz, M., Muller, D., Santorelli, S. F. *et al.* (2003).
140 Shah A.H., Joshi S.V., Mehrotra P.P., Potdar N, Dhar H.L. (2001).
141 See Chabot, D. (2000).

their curriculum not to mention that many classrooms are often unattractive, may have uncomfortable seating, and may even emit unpleasant odours. One project the teacher and students may do is to create a more aesthetic environment for their classroom conducive to triggering physiopleasure.

It seems to me that the most important would be for the teacher to incorporate physiopleasure in his teaching curriculum. For instance, he could have students move around, put some music on, stimulate the senses by having fun with original presentations for example. It has been shown that physiopleasure such as pleasant smells[142], music, and massage[143] were involved in a greater activation of the left prefrontal lobe.

We ought not to forget that the emotional learning process is associative. In other words, the memory of a situation can trigger an emotion. But the opposite is also true; the memory of an emotion can trigger the memory of a situation. For example, if the teacher plays a soft music when he teaches a subject, then invites the students to listen to it when they study, and finally plays that same music again during an exam, it is possible that this may stimulate the recurrence of the declarative memories that are linked to the memory of the class subject learned.

Conversely, it is important to understand that if physiopleasure exists then so does physiopain. And because this is the case, their negative impact on the learning process is undeniable. To put it more accurately, though this may displease some of you, most high schools and colleges have a complete lack of physiopleasure. In other words, these institutions lack sensuality. Their "clinical" design often provides nothing for the senses; concrete and steel construction, lack of color, limited natural light, and aesthetic visual concepts. Quite often, the graffiti written by students on these walls demonstrate their feeling of being "jailed" rather than expressing their desire to learn and the pleasure they should feel in developing themselves. This is unfortunate because we think that the lack of physiopleasure in these environments contributes to the high rate of vandalism in hallways, restrooms, and classrooms. Thus, the lack of beauty and harmony leads to aggressiveness and destruction. And this is certainly not conducive to a learning environment.

Therefore, we feel that it is important to address this issue if we truly want to optimize the learning and integration conditions at school.
The table below shows examples of physiopleasure. Feel free to add more :

---

142 John P.K., Blackhart G.C., Woodward, K.M. Williams S.R. and Schwartz G.E.R. (2000).
143 Jones N.A., Field T. (1999).

Chapter 4

Table 4.9
Examples of physiopleasure

Senses	Description
Sound	Play soft music during classes and exercises
Sight	Decorate the classroom and move everything around on a regular basis
	Wear clothes that have a connection to the subject taught (ex : a history class with clothes that represent that time period)
Smell	Put some fragrances and perfumes in class
Touch	Invite students to massage each other's shoulders and upper body for a change and so that they can relax in periods of intense stress.

2. Sociopleasure deals with the pleasures of interpersonal relations, birthday celebrations, and discussions with others. In short, it includes any activity that involves verbal exchanges with other people.

The cooperative teaching and learning becomes very important at this point[144]. In addition, there are numerous ways in which sociopleasure can be stimulated in schools. For instance, when a student works or interacts with another student, they both feel sociopleasure. However, if students that are interacting are not vigilant and interpersonal conflicts arise, then this sociopleasure can quickly turn to sociopain.

This is why the teacher must organize his curriculum in such a way that collaborations between students (such as open forums, discussions, and friendly debates) are encouraged. And the students' profiles will be able to tell who is in a greater need for sociopleasure (this is normally the case for students who have a high dependence for reward). Thus, if a teacher can stimulate the sociopleasure of students in need then the value and quality of his teaching methods are enhanced many fold.

A study conducted on 48 children has shown that those who have the best social competency (initiative and positive affect) also had a greater activity of the left prefrontal lobe compared to the children who show social withdrawal characteristics thus, a greater activity of the right prefrontal lobe[145].

Table 4.10 shows some examples of sociopleasure. Feel free to add more :

---

144 See Howden, J. and Kopiec, M. (2000).
145 Fox N.A., Rubin K.H., Calkins S.D., Marshall T.R., Coplan R.J., Porges S.W., Long J.M., Stewart S. (1995).

Managing emotions

Table 4.10
Examples of sociopleasure

Description
Team work
Discussion sessions
Class activities adapted to the students' interests and related to class subjects
Treat the class as a team and select a team's captain
Apply the teaching and learning methods according to the class project

3. Psychopleasure deals with activities that seek self-accomplishment and self-realization. They are very personal and cover different activities such as attending a College, learning a profession, traveling, doing odd jobs, playing a musical instrument, being part of a theatre company, et cetera.

Nourishing our psychopleasure is similar to nourishing our motivation. In other words, the more the teacher stimulates the student in his quest for self-accomplishment and the pursuit of his goals, the more this will contribute to the stimulation of his psychopleasure and therefore increase his chances of being successful in life. Consequently, it is essential for the school environment to be one of psychopleasure because the very nature of any academic approach is for the students to accomplish something in life. Unfortunately, the school and education system only stifle psychopleasure. For too long now it has been emphasized that school was not a place to have fun. This is a serious mistake that can have consequences not only on the students' motivation to go to school but more importantly on the learning process itself.

Each time we are in contact with a source of pleasure that can have a bearing on self-development, on the surpassing of oneself, or on the accomplishment of something for oneself, we are more likely to feel the psychopleasure.

Table 4.11 shows some examples of psychopleasure. Feel free to add more :

Table 4.11
Examples of psychopleasure

Description
Invite students to identify their dreams and passions
Invite students to identify the link between the subject that you teach them and the dreams that they pursue
Invite students to identify what they have accomplished up until now insofar as the pursuit of their academic and personal goals
Invite students to identify what it is at school that helps them to develop
Favor a teaching and learning method according to projects associated to the class subject studied

Chapter 4

4. Ideopleasure deals with the psyche, internal beauty, and even spirituality. They cover all the pleasure of reflection, creativity (artistically or scientifically), contemplation, meditation, philosophy, and prayer. Actually, ideopleasure cover the existential and spiritual dimension of human beings, their quest for a meaning, for an understanding, and for progress.

We can consider that ideopleasure are grouped into three categories of existential needs :

<u>The need for one's life to have a meaning</u>. Every human being needs to feel that is life his meaningful. When we take a look at the different cultures that populate this planet, we realize that there are many ways in which a human being's quest for a meaning can be defined. Every culture, every People, and all the great traditions try to bring a purpose to life, a reason for living, and a meaning to many of the great questions that call for our conscience such as : Why life? Why death? Why suffering? Why poverty? Why wars?. These questions are universal and even students ask them. Hence, a school environment is a great place to address these issues, not so much to find answers but more importantly to provide an environment that will encourage students to openly address these questions. This need to find a meaning to life is certainly not foreign to the high suicide rate amongst teenagers. Moreover, researchers from the Center for the Advancement of Health have shown that the quest for a purpose in life can improve our immune system[146] as well as the quality of life amongst the elderly[147].

<u>The need to contribute to life</u>. Every human being needs to feel that he contributes to life. Not only do we need to feel that our life has a meaning, but also that what we do in life, the reason why we study or work is part of something greater than ourselves. Hence, when we have the feeling that we contribute to life, we increase our chances of finding motivation. Otherwise, we feel that we are wasting our time and not accomplishing anything. Therefore, it is important to feel that we contribute to life. Once again, school plays a great role in that respect. Indeed, the teacher must constantly remind students of their importance in the world and that when they lose sight of this notion, they may become discouraged and not be able to regain happiness in their lives. The teacher must be mindful of the important role he plays to that effect because, too often, he unconsciously undermines this need so important to the students. It is evident that students who are passionate about the dream of contributing to something noble will be endowed with an unshakable motivation and will easily be able to pass through the pitfalls and difficulties of life.

<u>The need to feel inner peace</u>. Every human being seeks serenity. However, what will enable humans to feel inner peace more than anything else lies in the first two previously mentioned existential needs. In other words, when we feel that our life has a meaning and that we contribute to life in some way, we then feel

---

146 See : http ://www.sciencedaily.com/releases/2003/04/030429083520.htm : Searching For Meaning In Life May Boost Immune System.
147 Krause N. (2003).

the inner peace and that what we are doing is worthwhile. There is nothing worse than simply working for a salary or for a grade and having the unenthusiastic thought of feeling useless or feeling that what we do has very little value.

Ideopleasure is, undoubtedly, the most neglected need of our education system yet, it is also the most important. When we feel that our life has a meaning, that we contribute to something greater than ourselves, and that we found inner peace, our desire to continue on that path can only grow. And in order to stimulate this need, teachers must have the ability to convey a more philosophical and existential dimension as to the place and role of the subjects covered in class, of the students' fields of study, of the dreams that students cherish in life, and their contributions as human beings in terms of social and humanitarian developments.

Table 4.12 shows some examples of ideopleasure. Feel free to add more :

Table 4.12
Examples of ideopleasure

Category	Description
The meaning of life	Invite each student to tell the class how they define 'meaning of life', why they come to school, how school can contribute to bringing a sense to life and more happiness, why they chose this class subject and how it can help them, et cetera.
The contribution to life	Ask students to ask themselves (alone or in a group) how they can, via their studies, contribute to life.
Feeling inner peace	Invite students to question their self-worth and to identify their qualities and strengths. Also ask them to identify and feel the good that they do around them.

Managing our emotions through meditation

There exist several meditation approaches and techniques. The one we are describing here is simple and efficient and does not allude to any beliefs. It simply focuses on 'self', on 'the moment', and on the contacts established with people around us. Table 4.13 describes a step-by-step guide to conduct a meditation. Before it starts, it is recommended for the teacher to turn the lights off. Then he invites students to sit in a very comfortable position and waits for a complete silence. And lastly, the teacher follows the instructions below :

Table 4.13
Step-by-step guide for a class meditation

Step	Example of a meditation
Step 1 Relaxing through breathing	I invite you to unwind and relax Close your eyes and loosen up Breathe a little bit more deeply than usual You breathing goes deeper and you feel more relaxed You breathe using your belly and without raising your shoulders Breathe in through the nose and out through the mouth Feel your belly inflate Think only of your breathing and nothing else You feel more and more stress-free, more and more relaxed The oxygen that travels to your lungs triggers a tingling in your body, your fingers, and your toes This same oxygen creates a light euphoric sensation in you (you repeat this process for a total of twenty breaths)
Step 2 Awareness of 'self'	You will now allow your breathing to come back to normal And you will take the time to think about yourself Be aware of who you are and of what composes you Think of your feet and the fact that they are resting on the floor Feel you feet, then your calves, and your thighs You really feel your thighs – from the tips of your toes to your hips Feel your hips, the base of your belly, your trunk, and your back Rid your mind of any thought. Just feel your body – from the tips of your toes to your shoulders Now think of your hands – imagine that you are your hands, your arms, all the way up to your shoulders Your are completely relaxed, stress-free, and invaded by a soothing sensation Now think of your face and feel all the parts of your face, your mouth, your cheeks, your nose, and your eyes Think of your entire body as a whole

Step 3 Awareness of others and our environment	Think of the people around you, your classmates You are sitting on your chair and you feel totally relaxed Imagine the other students sitting around you and how relaxed they are too Think of all the people who are in this school Imagine everyone being calm just like you Now take it a little broader and imagine all the people who live in this city, this state, this country, and finally everywhere on this planet Think of the fact that you are one person among thousands and thousands That you are one person living on planet Earth and there are billions of people on this planet Just becoming aware of this makes you feel better already It allows you to communicate better with others and to remain at peace It allows you to respect and appreciate yourself more It helps you feel better, listen to yourself and to others more
Step 4 End of the meditation	Now you will start moving your toenails and fingernails slightly Then, you will slowly open your eyes and look at your classmates around you Stretch yourself like cats do and feel the benefits of this meditation

This is all! Now you can begin your class in harmony and joy. It is very possible that students may laugh at the beginning but after a while, you will see, they will beg for it.

* * *

In this chapter, we have explored how to help students better manage emotions that hinder the learning process. Firstly, we have emphasized the importance of empathy and compassion, and overemphasized the notion that any person that wants to help another person must be endowed with these two great human qualities. Secondly, we went through all the steps that characterize emotional intelligence such as identification, expression, understanding, and emotional management. We covered how empathetic listening was indispensable when it comes to helping a student identify and express his emotions. Then, we explored in greater details, the management of emotions by breaking down each component of an emotion. We saw how to manage nonverbal expressions, and physiological as well as behavioral reactions. In the same manner, we addressed the management of cognitions and irrational needs by describing the APEI method, a method designed to help students progress toward a more efficient

Chapter 4

approach. Then we mentioned the management of background emotions by highlighting the different sources of pleasure that a person can feel : physiopleasure, sociopleasure, psychopleasure, and ideopleasure. And finally, we have described the most powerful way to stimulate our left prefrontal lobe, through meditation.

In the next chapter, we will explore the other side of emotional pedagogy, the one that helps the student to feel the emotions that favor learning.

Chapter 5

Stimulating the emotions that are favorable to the learning process

T his is where any teacher's greatest challenge lies. He must be able to stimulate the student in a way that will help him feel the emotions that are favorable to the learning process and, therefore, help him better feel what he is learning. This puts us at the very heart of the notion of 'motivation'. We know that approximately 30 percent of Quebec high school students do not complete their high school program, and that 40 percent of students do not complete their college program, and finally, that 45 percent of students do not complete their university program[148]. We also know that the problem is more prevalent in men than in women.

But the most relevant aspect for us, at this point, is to realize that it is not because a student gets the results that we expect of him that he really learned how to get them. In other words, it is not because a student finds a solution to a problem that he necessarily learned something. As a general rule, the teacher will presuppose that if a student finds the right answer, it is because he knows how to find it. The truth of the matter is that perhaps the student knows how to find the right answer but this does not imply that deep inside he truly feels that he knows how to find it. How many times have you been able to achieve something and later wondered how you did it? And maybe you even were complimented for it yet you felt awkward inside because you did not really feel that you understood how you did it, i.e., that you were incompetent.

---

148 According to Vallerand, R. J. (1993), p. 533-581.

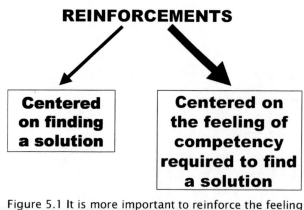

REINFORCEMENTS

| Centered on finding a solution | Centered on the feeling of competency required to find a solution |

Figure 5.1 It is more important to reinforce the feeling of competency required to find a solution rather than simply reinforce the search for a solution alone.

Hence, there is a distinguishing difference that requires further explanation. In general, any teacher will reward (or reinforce) the student every time he finds the correct answer and in that case we will say that the reward focuses more on the search for a solution. However, our approach goes one step further. It does not totally ignore the reinforcement of compliments for finding the right answer, but rather emphasizes the attainment by the student of a feeling of competency. In other words, the reinforcement will emphasize the feeling of competency more so than simply the search for a solution alone (see figure 5.1).

Here is an important assertion to consider :

The use of reinforcements that aim at making the student feel competent will result in generating a feeling that he can truly find a solution to a problem or accomplish a task. Conversely, the reinforcements that only seek to have the student look for a solution (or accomplish a task) for the sole purpose of getting rewarded with reinforcing compliments if he succeeds, do not give him the incentive to try to master the task. Instead, it encourages him to accomplish the task only to get rewarded and approved by the teacher[149].

Numerous studies have shown the extent to which it was important to adapt the learning process around the feeling of competency rather than just on finding the right solution. And these studies have also confirmed that the consequences of such an approach were positive for the learning process, academic performance, creativity, and perseverance at school[150].

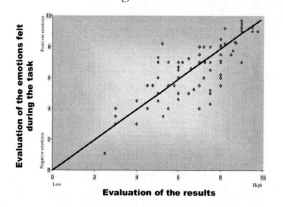

Figure 5.2 Correlation between the emotions felt during the accomplishment of a task and the evaluation of the results obtained during the task.

It is noteworthy that the feeling of competency is directly linked to our emotions. Indeed, within the scope of our seminars on emotional intelligence, we have made an interesting observation. When a group of individuals (or an individual) carry out a task, their perception of success while they are carrying out the task is directly linked to the emotions that they feel during its accomplishment. Figure 5.2 clearly shows the correlation ($r = 0.79$, $p < 0.0001$) that exists between the emotions felt during the

---

149 See Pelletier, L. G. and Vallerand, R. J. (1993).
150 According to Vallerand, R. J. (1993).

Chapter 5

accomplishment of a task and the level of satisfaction for the results obtained as the task was being carried out. In one exercise, a total of 109 subjects were involved in trying to solve an enigma. Several groups of ten to 12 people were formed and each group was given thirty clues to solve the enigma, which consisted of answering six questions. After the exercise was over, each participant had to fill out the evaluation form shown on figure 5.3 by first identifying the emotions that they felt and then answering the questions on their personal (emotional) evaluation and the evaluation of the results. The average for each of the two different sections was very similar (personal evaluation = 6.62/10 and evaluation of the results = 6.19/10). This observation indicates that the better the participants felt during the exercise of solving the enigma, the

more satisfied they were with the results, no matter what these were. This point is very relevant because when the participants filled out the form, they did not yet know how many good answers they would get out of the six questions from the enigma. And it is only after they filled out the form (on figure 5.3) that the answers to the enigma were given to them. Hence, all the teams involved in this exercise learned during the correction of the enigma that they received five out of six good answers i.e. 83 percent. However, the average of their evaluation of the results was 6.19/10 i.e. 62 percent, which means 21 percent below the 83 percent. It is clear that this lower percentage is a reflection of the emotions they felt during the exercise. In other words, our own perception and judgment can be altered by our emotions as described in chapter 2.

These results confirm that the better we feel, the more we can appreciate our results, no matter what they are. However, reality tells us that it is not always simple to constantly feel pleasure when we learn. Learning is not always easy and it would be fallacious to believe or pretend that we can eliminate all forms of pain during the learning process. The fact is that learning requires effort, arduous work, and

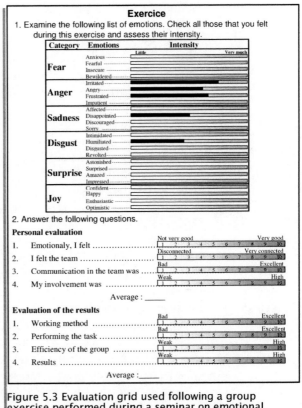

Figure 5.3 Evaluation grid used following a group exercise performed during a seminar on emotional intelligence. Each participant individually filled out the form. Then, the group average for the two sections Personal (emotional) evaluation and Evaluation of the results was compiled.

takes place on a road filled with pitfalls. Hence, despite the fact that teachers and students alike are aware that the hardships of learning are a well-known reality, it would be a mistake to turn away from this reality without taking advantage of it. If our goal is to learn in a pleasurable environment and to stimulate our pleasure for learning, then we must, first and foremost, address the notion of pain found in many learning methods. Yet, this notion of pain can easily turn into pleasure if we know how to take advantage of emotional 'metacompetency' "a method that uses our emotions and our basic emotional competencies". The next section of this chapter will explain how to achieve it. To do so, however, we will address a very interesting theory developed by Richard Solomon : the theory of antagonistic processes[151].

The antagonistic processes

The theory of antagonistic processes allows us to understand certain behaviors that are seemingly contradictory. In general, any theory on motivation says that we have a tendency to seek situations that are pleasurable and to avoid situations that are not. In fact, there are many examples that describe this learning process and that are based on what is commonly termed "behavioral or operand conditioning". Basically, operand conditioning occurs when a response to a stimulus is either positively or negatively reinforced. More specifically, our behavior tends to increase when we are positively reinforced (reward) and decrease when we are negatively reinforced (punishment). Interestingly, there are many examples of behaviors that do not follow this model such as when a negative reinforcement sustains a certain behavior. Here are some examples :

> ➢ A woman who finds it very difficult to leave her partner despite the many fights they have, and the violence that she is subjected to;
> ➢ A person who loses a lot of money at the casino but continues to gamble regardless;
> ➢ A person who does parachuting despite the intense fear that he feels;
> ➢ A person who is addicted to drugs despite the harsh side effects that they generate.

In these four examples, we can describe two versions of the theory of antagonistic processes. The first version has to do with situations which bring a great deal of pleasure at first, but then gradually turn into pain. Such is the case with two people beginning a new relationship, experiencing pleasure and passion. Over time, the amount of pain exceeds the pleasurable moments. The same phenomenon occurs when a person becomes addicted to drugs. In the beginning, it is extremely pleasurable to use these substances but as time goes by the person suffers tremendous side effects and becomes dependent.

The other version goes through the opposite process. At first, the person derives pain from the situation but eventually enjoys it and becomes addicted. For example, people who go parachuting tend to be very scared at first when it is time to jump. But with time, this fear gives way to an intense pleasure or thrill. The same phenomenon occurs with gamblers or compulsive wagers who lose money more often than they win. Despite the fact that the pain triggered by the losses is more frequent than the pleasure triggered by the wins, the latter still remains immeasurably significant in the eyes of the gambler for the reasons that will be explained below.

---

151 Solomon, R.L. (1980).

According to the theory of antagonistic processes, each time a stimulus triggers an intense positive (pleasure) or negative (pain) emotion in any given situation, an opposite reaction takes place and tends to replace that initial emotion as soon as the situation changes or ends.

Each time a stimulus is felt by an individual, it either triggers a pleasant affective reaction or an unpleasant one. This process occurs in four distinct steps :

a. The initial reaction reaches a peak;
b. An adaptation phase takes place and creates a decrease in the intensity of the initial sensation;
c. When the stimulus disappears, an opposite affective reaction occurs;
d. After some time, the affective state returns to its basal level.

Figure 5.4 describes the phenomenon based on a situation that is extremely pleasant at first. Let us take the example of a person who uses an exhilarating drug such as cocaine. He will feel an intense pleasure at first and after an antagonistic adaptation process, the initial pleasure will rapidly fade away. This same antagonistic process will create an opposite sensation and give way to pain brought about by the disappearing effect of the substance.

As the situation becomes more and more familiar, the person becomes accustomed to it and an habituation mechanism takes place. This habituation mechanism ensures that the initial pleasure becomes less intense and that the pain that follows becomes more intense (see figure 5.5). This is precisely what happens when a person uses drugs. In the beginning, the user feels a euphoric effect brought about by the use of the drug. Then his motivation becomes the consumption of that drug for the pleasure that it brings. But with time, the habituation phenomenon called "drug addiction tolerance" leads the user to feel less and less pleasure with using the drug and more pain when not using it. Hence, his motivation for using the drug progresses from a consumption behavior based on pleasure to

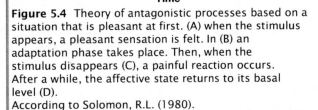

Figure 5.4 Theory of antagonistic processes based on a situation that is pleasant at first. (A) when the stimulus appears, a pleasant sensation is felt. In (B) an adaptation phase takes place. Then, when the stimulus disappears (C), a painful reaction occurs. After a while, the affective state returns to its basal level (D).
According to Solomon, R.L. (1980).

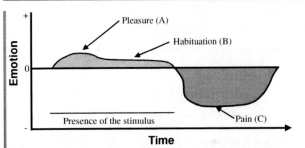

Figure 5.5 When the situation comes back, the initial pleasure (A) becomes less intense because of the habituation process (B). However, the pain that follows the absence of the stimulus becomes more intense (C).

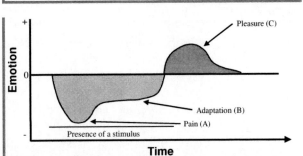

Figure 5.6 Theory of antagonistic processes based on a situation that is unpleasant at first. An intense pain is felt (A) when the stimulus occurs. Then comes the adaptation phase (B) where the intensity of the pain decreases. Finally, when the stimulus disappears, an intense pleasure appears (C).
Adapted from Mook, D.G. (1987).

Stimulating emotions

a consumption behavior based on the elimination of pain.

The explanation described above not only applies to the use of drugs but also to loving relationships. Indeed, during these relationships lovers seek the presence of their partner for the intense pleasure that it brings in the beginning. But as habits emerge from the relationship and as the relationship declines, shunning the pain of being alone or not feeling the presence of one's partner becomes more important than enjoying the pleasure of being together.

The theory of antagonistic processes also explains why initially disheartening and unpleasant situations can become exciting and coveted. Imagine, for instance, the emotions that you would feel if you were to go parachuting for the first time in your life. Figure 5.6 clearly illustrates what happens. The initial pain and fear (A) are very intense but quickly fade and give way to an adaptation phase. And when the unpleasant stimulus disappears, another rebound of pleasure (B) occurs. In the case of parachuting, the fear that is felt in the beginning is very strong. But it gradually lessens and gives way to the pleasure that is felt when the parachute opens up or when the person lands on the ground safely.

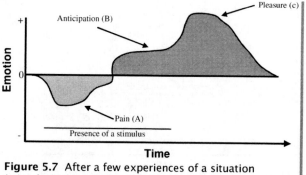

Figure 5.7 After a few experiences of a situation (stimulus), the initial pain (A) leads to an anticipated pleasure (B) followed by an intense pleasure (C), shortly after the stimulus disappeared. This experience ultimately leads to a euphoric sensation even though it started with an initial pain
Adapted from Mook, D.G. (1987)

In short, the more frequently that we experience a situation and the weaker the initial pain becomes, over time, the experience itself will give way to a certain pleasure and feeling of well-being. Figure 5.7 shows that the pain (A) following the experience is shorter and less intense. This initial pain quickly turns into an anticipated pleasure, followed by an intense euphoric feeling and a return to a normal state. Douglas Mook[152] explains that any organic imbalance creates a behavior that seeks to restore that balance. In other words, the moment an intense emotional experience disrupts our psychological and physiological equilibrium, a compensatory force (antagonistic emotion) seeks to restore it[153]. This compensatory process is essentially what we must rely on in order to counter the difficulties of learning. Indeed, any learning method has its highly sought after pleasant moments and its undesired unpleasant moments. And the latter are perhaps the ones that lead to different sorts of inadequate behaviors such as disengagement, inhibition, and withdrawal.

Any individual who successfully goes through a rigorous learning process has also managed to overcome and adapt to the pitfalls along the way. Some people even become masters at this while others struggle tremendously. We feel that the success essentially lies in the ability to transform the anguish of the learning

152 Mook, D.G. (1987).
153 Huffman, K., M. Vernoy and J. Vernoy (2000).

method with the anticipated pleasure of successfully going through the learning method itself. In fact, as we mentioned before, the feeling of competency is acquired not just when the desired result is attained but also when we can manage the difficulties encountered along the way. This is another challenge for both the educator and the learner.

The antagonistic processes in learning

The antagonistic processes apply to any type of learning approach. Indeed, when we are exposed to a new learning method, we quickly encounter difficulties or pains that we must overcome through determination otherwise they can trigger a desire to give up. Any success will, in turn, prevail over the difficulties of the learning approach. In that sense, it is clear that two ingredients are needed for this to happen; a resolute will to persist over the pains that come with the implicit learning effort, and successes along the way so as to eliminate the pains of the learning effort. Without these successes, the determination and persistence will weaken and eventually fade completely, and this will ultimately lead to a desire to drop out. In fact, even the highest level of determination must be reinforced regularly with occasional successes. This means that the determination of the student must be stimulated and his successes must be regularly highlighted.

In the previous section, we made an assertion to the effect that it was more important to reinforce a feeling of competency than to simply find a solution. Here is another important assertion, which applies to Solomon's theory of antagonistic processes :

Any teacher must be able to stimulate two things in the student :

> 1. His determination, by encouraging and helping him to deal with the pains of the learning approach;
> 2. His feeling of competency, by highlighting each little success that will ultimately leads to the final result.

In short, determination leads to success and success nurtures determination. As shown on figure 5.8, the antagonistic process gradually leads the learner to avoid the difficulties encountered but also to search for them as he knows that these difficulties will be conquered successfully. Thus, the learning process takes place in two ways; through the cognitive or technical learning of the subject itself and through the emotional learning that lies beneath the cognitive or technical learning. This means that the cognitive or technical learning depends mainly on the

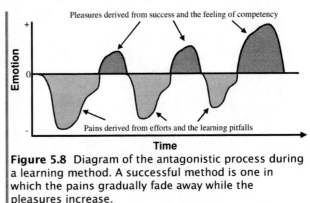

Figure 5.8 Diagram of the antagonistic process during a learning method. A successful method is one in which the pains gradually fade away while the pleasures increase.

emotional learning which is present throughout the process. Without this, any cognitive or technical learning approach will be compromised. Paradoxically, emotional learning relies, in part, on how the cognitive or technical learning will be processed. Indeed, if the learner does not experience any successes, or if they are not highlighted and they do not stimulate his feeling of competency then the learning process can potentially end prematurely.

Benefiting from the antagonistic processes during emotional pedagogy

We have already outlined that positive emotions can facilitate the learning process while negative ones can hinder it. Therefore, taking advantage of the antagonistic processes means to be mindful that any learning approach must go through pain and pleasure phases. This means that the road to success can only be guaranteed by acknowledging the little pleasures brought about by the little successes. The teacher must therefore be aware of the importance of highlighting these successes when they occur. He must pay close attention to the choice of their students' learning method, which can be a difficult task especially when there are many students. The teacher must also tell students that they too have an important role to play such as knowing about each other's learning method and being able to recognize their own successes.

Below is an exercise that we encourage you to do with your students at the end of an important learning step, exercise, or evaluation. You will notice that this exercise is an application of the APIE method[154] described in chapter 4.

---

154 the Affect, the Predominantly difficult, the Irrational need and the Emergence.

Exercise 5.1
Evaluation of one's learning method

By referring to the table below, try to identify the emotions that you felt during the subject covered in class or during the exercise that you did or the exam that you just took. Also try to quantify these emotions using the scale on the right.

Category	Emotions	Intensity
		Little ——————————————————— Very much
Fear	Affraid-------------	
	Worried------------	
	Timid--------------	
	Insecure -----------	
	Bewildered --------	
Anger	Annoyed------------	
	Irritated------------	
	Frustrated----------	
	Impatience---------	
	Angry--------------	
Sadness	Bored--------------	
	Disappointed-------	
	Discouraged--------	
	Sorry--------------	
	Sad----------------	
Disgust	Bitterness----------	
	Humiliated---------	
	Be reluctant to------	
	Intimidated--------	
	Disgusted----------	
Contempt	Contempt-----------	
	Discredit-----------	
	Underestimated-----	
	Revolted-----------	
Surprise	Astonished---------	
	Surprise------------	
	Amazed------------	
	Impressed----------	
Joy	Happy--------------	
	Confident----------	
	Content------------	
	Enthusiastic--------	
	Optimistic---------	

Stimulating emotions

What did you find the most difficult in this situation? In other words, was there a moment when you felt bad and, if so, describe that moment? (ex : when the teacher discussed such topic I didn't understand and felt stupid because it looked as though everyone else understood except me.)

During that moment (from #2), what did you wish would have happened for you to feel better?
(ex : I would have liked for the teacher to realize that I did not understand; or for me to have the courage to tell him that I no longer understood what he was saying.)

In the previously described situation, try to specify at what moment you experienced success or pleasure (however minor), and what emotion or feeling you felt at that time.
(ex : Up to a certain point, I felt good because I understood what the teacher was saying; or when I worked on this part of the exercise or the exam, I felt that things were going well; or when the teacher came to me to see if everything was going well, I felt his support.)

When you think back about this success, how do you feel?
(ex : It makes me feel good because I realize that I'm not as dumb as I thought; or it reassures me because I then realize that not everything is bad; or I feel reassured to see that the teacher cares about my success.)

Describe how this success or pleasure can help you learn the class subject or simply help you complete your class.
(ex : The fact that it gives me confidence in my ability to succeed even if I don't like the subject ; or if things don't go well, at least the teacher is there to help me.)

----

* * *

In short, Solomon's theory of antagonistic processes allows us to understand the true meaning of pleasure, however small, and its significance in the learning process. Learning inevitably involves having to face difficulties, doubts, and even despair. Thus, it would be unrealistic to think that it can be done effortlessly and

Chapter 5

painlessly. Conversely, it is also unrealistic to think that it is impossible to learn and experience successes and moments of joy and well-being.

Any success and/or pleasure that are experienced during any learning process are the antidote to losing the inner drive to learn. And it is not just dropping out of school, as is generally the case, but also dropping out of the inner drive to learn. Any individual has a need to feel connected to any form of pleasure that relates to his learning approach, and feel positive when he is learning. Otherwise, any disconnection from these pleasures will inexorably lead him to give up, fail, or dropout.

You can even ask your friends how much they enjoy learning. Ask them what they like to feel when they learn something new. You will discover that they all have different answers. Some need to feel support from their teacher while some need to understand the higher purpose for what they do. Others feel the importance of experiencing little successes along the way while others feel good only if they understand everything as a whole. Your observations will help you understand that some like it only when it is novel and different, while others only when it is familiar and routine. Perhaps your experience as a teacher has also allowed you to come across students who appeared stoic when you mentioned that they may fail their semester, whereas others reacted very strongly. Similarly, you may have observed that some students were seeking your approval and your support while other students were insensitive to it.

In the next chapter, we will further discuss individual differences that exist between students. We will describe the role played by personality traits with students' individual methods of learning and their diverse manner of addressing successes and failures. In other words, we all react differently to pains and pleasures, to reinforcements and punishments, to the anticipation of positive and negative events, et cetera.

Chapter 6

Personality profiles, teacher/pupil relationships, and the learning process

As we have already outlined several times, we maintain that the true learning process takes place when we are in the 'feeling' mode. Having said that, it is obvious that not everyone feel things the same way, i.e., that there exist many different ways of 'feeling' things. Indeed, we all have different feelings about 0life's situations and, consequently, the things we learn from the different situations that we are confronted with are very different. Hence, the way to feel and react to stimuli from our environment will differ considerably from one individual to another, and will have an impact on our ways of learning. Therefore, it is important for the teacher to recognize a few notions related to personality traits in order to know how to apply them to emotional pedagogy.

The three biological dimensions of personality

Neuropsychiatrist Robert Cloninger has been working specifically on the psychobiological basis of personality[155]. Although, his model is relatively complex in its entirety[156], the elements that we have kept are easy to understand. Thanks

---

155 Cloninger C.R., Svrakic D.M., Przybeck T.R. (1993).
156 Currently, Robert Cloninger's model has two dimensions : one is innate, which represents the temperament, and the other one is acquired and represents the character. Cloninger identified four temperament traits : researching novelty, avoiding punishment, need for reward, and persistence. Cloninger also identified three chatacter traits : self-control, cooperation, and self-transcendence.

to Cloninger's precious work, we were able to develop nine personality profiles[*]. These profiles rely on three personality components :

> **Need to seek novelty**, i.e., seeking new stimulations;
> **Need to avoid punishment and pain**, i.e., tendency to respond intensely to aversive stimuli or adopt behaviors designed to avoid punishment;
> **Need for reward and affection**, i.e., tendency to respond intensely to reward stimuli and learn to maintain a reinforced behavior or remain firm when it is no longer there.

Now, let us examine each of these personality traits that, according to Cloninger, are innate, for the most part, and rely on a particular neurological functioning.

Need to seek novelty

Individuals whose search for novelty is highly developed usually have a strong need for new sensations. They normally seek everything that can stimulate, interest, and invigorate them. They enjoy experimenting with new things and taking physical risks as well as risks in their social and emotional relationships.

However, they also have a tendency to be impulsive and disorganized, and to get bored easily when things become routine. The advantage for people who seek novelty and have this type of strong temperament trait is that they are very enthusiastic and are quick to get involved in anything that is new. They love change and are very curious.

On the other hand, they are often fiery and become easily frustrated when their desires or needs are not met. Thus, they have a tendency to be fickle when things require an effort, and even their relationships are often unstable and agitated.

Conversely, individuals who have less of a need to seek novelty are generally less curious and enthusiastic, less expressive, and more reserved and rigid. They are comfortable with routine and monotony, and are more stable in their work and relationships. In addition, they are also very patient and do not become frustrated easily.

Additionally, these individuals are generally thoughtful, tidy, methodical, and well organized. Their weakness is simply that they take time before committing to new ideas or new approaches, and they usually feel destabilized when their habits are threatened.

In short, spontaneous novelty seekers have an intense need (above average) for emotional stimulations. This need can be explained by low levels of dopamine in

---

* We are currently the first authors to propose these nine personality profiles. More specialized trainings on these profiles are offered by the Academy of Pleasurology and Emotional Intelligence (APEI) (see www.apie.ca) and by the Emotional Pedagogy Institute (see www.emotionalpedagogy.com).

Chapter 6

certain areas of the brain[157]. Dopamine is a neurotransmitter in the brain and is linked to pleasure and activation. Because dopamine levels are chronically insufficient in these individuals, they have a tendency to compensate this deficiency by seeking anything that can stimulate their sense of pleasure and generate an activation state. This also means that these individuals are at a higher risk for drug addiction, alcoholism, and impulsive behaviors such as extreme sports, gambling, and delinquency.

When students in a classroom have a strong need for novelty and need higher levels of stimulation, they need to become energized, and involved in their learning. Consequently, if the teacher can engage them into becoming interested, then they will become involved and focused. But if the teacher is boring and unexciting, they will certainly lose interest and will more than likely dropout. An interesting study has shown that dropout students had a high score in the novelty-seeking scale developed by Robert Cloninger[158].

Conversely, students who do not need as much novelty can endure monotony and concentrate on their task for a long time. They are stable and do not like to be disturbed from their routine and familiar situations. Contrary to their counterparts, these students become destabilized when new ideas or new approaches are presented to them. What this all means is that every new teaching approach that is used year after year does not necessarily fit with all the different students' profiles. In other words, some love novelty while others despise it.

Table 6.1 illustrates the characteristics of those students possessing a faint need for seeking novelty and those students with a strong need for seeking novelty.

Table 6.1
Characteristics of seeking novelty

Faint	Strong
Limited curiosity and limited enthusiasm Limited expressiveness, reserved and rigid Tolerate routine and monotony Thoughtful, tidy, methodical, and well organized Slow to commit to new ideas or approaches Patient and do not become frustrated easily Feel destabilized with change Stable in their work and relationships	Strong need for new sensations and stimulations Take physical risks Take risks in their relationships Impulsive and disorganized Do not tolerate routine Become easily bored in routine Enthusiastic and passionate Commit quickly Love change, are curious and open Impulsive and frustrated when desires are not met Fickle when an effort is required Unstable and agitated relationships

---

157 Souccar, T. (2001).
158 Wingerson D., Sullivan M., Dager S., Flick S., Dunner D., Roy-Byrne P. (1993).

Need to avoid punishment and pain

Individuals who have a dominating temperament trait for avoiding punishment and pain are usually cautious, anxious, and timid. They have a tendency to be pessimistic and to dread failure and adversity. They also have a hard time with uncertainty and unfamiliar situations, i.e., they are afraid of the unknown even when there is no need to be. Therefore, they are not risk-takers.

In their social relationships, they are shy and have no self-confidence. In other words, they tend to avoid meetings with strangers and need tangible signs of acceptance from them before establishing a contact. In addition, these individuals' energy level is low and they are often tired.

The advantage of this trait is that it leads these individuals to pay more attention to hazardous situations and better plan things. On the other hand, the disadvantage is that these individuals are needlessly timid.

Conversely, individuals who do not tend to avoid punishment and pain are often carefree, relaxed, and bold. They are optimistic, even in situations that others qualify as disturbing, are daring, open to others, and extroverted. Other features that these individuals have are high-energy, liveliness, and vitality.

In conclusion, individuals who seek to avoid punishment and pain are generally shy, fearful of pain, socially inhibited, and have little energy. This personality trait is apparently linked to high levels of serotonine; a neurotransmitter that acts as an inhibitor in several regions of the brain. Thus, someone with high levels of serotonine has inhibited behaviors and seeks to avoid pain[159]. Teenagers who show similar personality traits generally use drugs to eliminate their inhibitions. Ecstasy, for instance, is a drug that lowers serotonine activity resulting in the users' higher tendency to socialize[160]. Perhaps, this is the reason why adolescents who are introverted have so much appreciation for this drug which turns out to be the drug of choice in raves[161].

Students, whose have strong traits for avoiding punishment and pain usually do not speak very much in class and are very shy. They also dread being scolded and are afraid of failure as well. A teacher who can see these traits in a student should help him overcome his fears by simply talking to him, bringing him comfort, and supporting him when he takes risks. He must be mindful that students with such attributes are at a higher risk for depression, especially when they experience a failure[162]. However, he must also keep in mind that his students can potentially react positively when dealing with a fear of failure. In other words, the threat of punishment can be a good tool with such students.

---

159 Hansenne M., Ansseau M. (1999).
160 Kalant H. (2001).
161 It is noteworthy that esctasy is a very popular drug amongst teenagers who manifest strong 'search-for-novelty' traits. See Dughiero G, Schifano F, Forza G. (2001).
162 Hansenne M., Reggers J., Pinto E., Kjiri K., Ajamier A., Ansseau M. (1999).

Chapter 6

Conversely, individuals who do not seek to avoid punishment and pain are extroverted, bold, and almost unreasonably optimistic. Their lack of concern can put them at a higher risk for failure. Yet this is the least of their worries. In addition, they tend to be unmoved when the teacher lectures or threatens them. In fact, any threat of "punishment" will have no effect on them whatsoever. Therefore, to make these students more sensitive, the teacher must look for another option.

Table 6.2 summarizes the characteristics of this personality attribute.

Table 6.2
Characteristics of avoiding punishment and pain

Faint	Strong
Carefree, relaxed, and bold Unreasonably optimistic Daring, open to others, and extroverted Confident when facing danger Rash Confident when facing uncertainty High-energy, liveliness, verve, and vitality	Cautious, anxious, and timid Tendency to be pessimistic Dread failure and adversity Have a hard time with uncertainty and unfamiliar situations Afraid of the unknown Not a risk-taker Shy and no self-confidence Avoid meetings with strangers Need tangible signs of acceptance from others Low energy and often tired Better planners

Need for reward and affection

Individuals who have a strong need for affection need approval, support, and reinforcement from others. They are usually warm, sensitive, devoted, and truly seek social and emotional contacts with others. Therefore, this makes them very good at establishing friendly and intimate contacts because they are very comfortable expressing their emotions and sensitivity. They are also empathetic and understanding of others.

The advantage of this trait is that these individuals are very sensitive to social signals. This makes it easier for them to establish warm and understanding social relationships.

The disadvantage, however, is that their search for attachment and affection can lead them to become easily influenced and lose their objectivity. And in the most extreme cases, it can even lead them to develop a significant emotional dependency.

Conversely, individuals whose need for affection is faint are rather cold, apathetic, and socially numb. They prefer to be alone and not communicate with others and, as a result, are distant and rarely establish chemistry with other people.

This means that when the need for affection is low, it allows individuals to remain objective and not have their behaviors shaded by their desire to please or feel accepted. On the other hand, the lack of sensitivity in these individuals makes communication with them difficult. Emotional relationships with them are very unlikely. These individuals even become egotistical and have a complete lack of empathy and compassion for others.

In short, individuals whose need for reward and affection is strong seek significant emotional ties and approval from others and are usually worried about not being liked or accepted. This trait is linked to a low level of noradrenaline; a neurotransmitter whose role is to modulate attention, learning, and essentially to maintain drive and the capacity for reward. For instance, an individual who has a low activity of the noradrenaline pathways in the brain will tend to adopt a compensatory behavior by seeking much more attention and emotional ties from others.

In a classroom, students with a strong need for reward and affection usually tend to seek the admiration of others, and especially the teacher's approval. This is why it is very important to teach them to develop self-confidence. Otherwise they become destabilized when they do not have the approval or emotional support of their peers and, more importantly, of their teacher. However, these students feed on rewards and are stimulated by success, good grades, and attention or approval. Thus, in the same way that individuals with a strong trait for avoiding punishment and pain dread the negative consequences of their actions, those with a strong need for reward and affection are very sensitive to the idea of losing what they have. In other words, while some are afraid to feel pleasure, others are afraid to miss out on it.

Conversely, students whose need for reward and affection is barely perceptible are rather cold and reserved. A good teacher must try to encourage them to maintain interpersonal relationships. In addition, the teacher must be aware that these students do not have the tendency to anticipate reward and this explains why they do not covet good grades, good scores, or good relationships with their teacher. Telling them that they will succeed if they apply themselves is not necessarily the best approach.

Table 6.3
Characteristics of the need for reward and affection

Faint	Strong
Cold and apathetic Socially insensitive Distant and lonely Communicate little Have little affinity with others Remain objective No desire to please or feel accepted Difficult to communicate with them Emotional relationships are very unlikely Egotistical Complete lack of empathy and compassion	Need for the approval of others Need for support and reward Warm, sensitive, and devoted Seek social and emotional contacts Establish friendly and intimate contacts easily Express emotions and feelings easily Empathetic and understanding Easily influenced Lose objectivity easily

The nine personality profiles

Cloninger's model has led us to the conception of nine personality profiles[163]. Each of these profiles has its own distinctive features, its emotional dynamics, and its ways of feeling and learning. Table 6.4 summarizes them in relation to the three personality traits described by Cloninger.

Table 6.4
The nine personality profiles

Personality traits	Need to seek novelty	Need to avoid punishment and pain	Need for reward and affection
Bold	Strong	Faint	Faint
Theatrical	Strong	Faint	Strong
Extreme	Strong	Strong	Faint
Clever	Strong	Strong	Strong
Meticulous	Faint	Strong	Faint
Affective	Faint	Faint	Strong
Docile	Faint	Strong	Strong
Hermit	Faint	Faint	Faint
Flexible	Average	Average	Average

163 It is important to note that Cloninger's tridimensional personality model has important clinical applications. Our goal here is to highlight the students' prominent traits (which we often encounter in classrooms) and describe a way to deal with them.

Personality profiles

Let us examine each profile one by one.

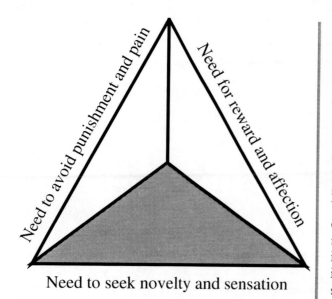

Need to avoid punishment and pain

Need for reward and affection

Need to seek novelty and sensation

The bold personality is characterized by a strong need to seek novelty, a faint need to avoid punishment and pain, and a faint need for reward and affection.

The profile of a student who is bold is the following. Considering that he has a faint need for reward and affection, he does not really seek contacts with others. Therefore, he has a tendency to be cold, distant, and lonely. He can also become egotistical and insensitive to others. Yet he is not a shy person. But even if he has no desire to establish contacts with others, he has no problem giving his advice if asked or partake in a group activity. He can even find enjoyment in shocking others by his behavior or offensive statements because his faint need to avoid punishment and pain and faint need for reward and affection will not make him fear controversy or rejection. On the contrary, it might even stimulate him.

In general, he has a lot of energy and vitality but gets bored quickly when things become monotonous. This is why school has the potential to bring little stimulation to him.

The mixture of a strong need for novelty and a faint need to avoid punishment and pain makes the individual susceptible to intense and even dangerous experiences. Given the fact that he likes to take risks and to make his experiences intense, he has plenty of nerve and is not afraid to get hurt. In addition, he is inclined to use drugs because he enjoys extreme sensations and is fearless. In fact, it takes a lot for him to get scared or to give up.

In general, he is the one who sits in the corner in the back of the class. He always works by himself because he does not seek contacts with others.

His profile makes him completely indifferent to threats of punishment or sanctions by the teacher. Most of all, he is almost never afraid of the teacher's authority or to find himself in a situation where he will have a failing grade.

Therefore, the best way to encourage antisocial students to learn is to stimulate them with new ideas. If, for instance, the teacher succeeds during his wonderful class to incorporate funny and surreal anecdotal situations then these types of students will generally respond well and their attention span will increase. In fact, during their group projects, these students must be encouraged to take different directions but be reminded of all the teaching goals that they will need to reach.

Also, when alone with an antisocial student, the teacher must be careful not to challenge him as he will not be easily intimidated. There is never much to gain when dealing with a bold student. On the contrary, the teacher must let him express his difference and encourage him to do the same for other students.

> The teacher should always remember three things when dealing with a student who is bold :
> - Sanctions do not work with him because he is not afraid of punishment and its consequences;
> - Charming him does not work either because he does not seek the approval of others nor does he care about establishing contacts with others;
> - Novel stimulations work very well with him because he is receptive to anything that can stimulate and surprise him.

The theatrical personality is characterized by a strong need to seek novelty, a faint need to avoid punishment and pain, and a strong need for reward and affection.

Hence, as the name indicates, the theatrical student is animated by a permanent need to exaggerate everything and put himself up on stage. His strong need to seek novelty makes him curious, open minded and passionate, and inclined to take risks in everything. In fact, all the components of novelty-seeking having to do with taking physical and relational risks and with the quest for adventure are heightened by a faint need to avoid punishment and pain. Indeed, the energy that is stored in him coupled with an unreasonable courage and carefree attitude when facing dangers make him a true daredevil who moves and talks relentlessly. Even when tired after long active periods, the theatrical student wants more.

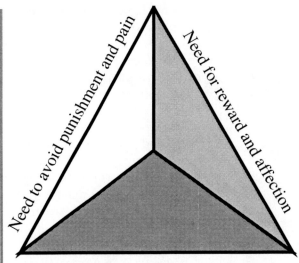

Furthermore, his strong need for reward and affection make him very sociable. The theatrical student is never alone. He knows hundreds of people and has many friends, is extroverted, and very open. The feeling that he conveys is that he knows everybody. Yet his is highly invigorated by a permanent desire to feel appreciated and to receive a great deal of attention from others.

He is generally easy to recognize at first glance. In a classroom, he is the one who talks the most in the very first class. He tells jokes, gets all the attention and, without hesitation, is always the first to answer questions from the teacher. In the beginning of the semester, when teachers invite students to introduce themselves, the theatrical student will surprise everyone by the way he expresses

Personality profiles

himself in front of the class and by the number of activities he is involved in. We have the feeling that he likes everything; sports, arts, all types of leisure activities, travel, nightclubs, et cetera.

Since he is unstable, restless, and even energized, this student is not easy to manage. On one hand, he makes others laugh and brings a relaxed atmosphere to the first classes. On the other hand, he can also tease and irritate others. For instance, in one of my communication classes in the beginning of the semester, I usually invite students to appoint a class leader. What is interesting is that, one after the other, all theatrical students suggest themselves as candidates or are quickly suggested by other non-theatrical students to become a class leader, and one of them is inevitably elected. However, when a similar exercise is conducted several weeks later, he is no longer elected. The reason is that his behavior towards others has created enough hostility to not have him as a leader a second time around.

Another interesting characteristic of the theatrical student is that he is a manipulator and will do anything to achieve his goal, even if it means over dramatizing a situation. He can be a pathological liar and tell absurd stories simply to gain your sympathy especially when he tries to avoid doing homework, or tries to justify missing a class or being late. He plays the victim or acts with kindness if chances are in his favor.

So the best way to deal with a theatrical character is to exploit another one of his traits. We already know that his faint need to avoid punishment and pain makes him insensitive to punishment. But we also know that his strong need for reward and affection will make him sensitive to the attention that you will give him. In other words, if punishment does not work well with him then reward will. He will come to appreciate the attention that you will give him and will react positively to any new experience.

Always remember three things with a student who has a theatrical profile :
- Sanctions do not work with him because he is not afraid of punishment and its consequences;
- Warm relationships and attention work because he seeks the approval of others and cares about establishing contacts with others;
- Novel stimulations work very well with him because he is receptive to anything that can stimulate and surprise him.

The extreme personality is characterized by a strong need to seek novelty, a strong need to avoid punishment and pain, and a faint need for reward and affection.

The interesting feature of the extreme student lies in the opposing nature of his profile. Indeed, since he has a strong need to seek novelty and a strong need to avoid punishment and pain, he is attracted by anything that is new but, at the same time, is very careful and insecure. In other words, he likes novelty but takes a lot of time before committing to new things because he needs to prepare and check many times if everything is secure and under control. As a result, he is constantly between two opposing forces, i.e., between the desire to take risks and live new

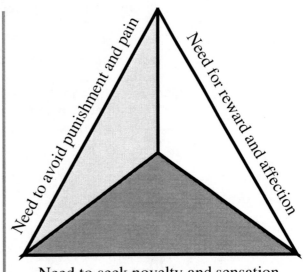

experiences on one hand, and the fear of taking risks and making the wrong choices on the other hand. In short, all the risks that he takes are calculated.

In his interpersonal relationships, the main components of his novelty-seeking feature to assess are his impulsive and unstable nature. This aspect is very important since the extreme student has a faint need for reward and affection. This means that communication is quite difficult to establish with him because he does not usually seek social contacts. Indeed, he has very little chemistry with others and is cold and distant. Moreover, his strong need to avoid punishment and pain makes him very anxious and incapable of tolerating situations that are stressful and unfamiliar. It takes a long time for him to recover from situations that are stressful and that require a great deal of energy.

Therefore, the extreme student has a difficult time tolerating the unknown. For example, when facing a difficult exercise, he becomes impulsive and his reaction is often exaggerated in relation to the significance of the situation. He may become angry and threaten to quit everything. Another feature is that his relationships are very unstable. Each time something goes wrong in his friendly and loving relationships, his emotions almost always go awry.

He may be unstable emotionally however his rational intelligence is generally very good. And the combination of both makes his academic life very difficult and tumultuous.

This type of reaction can compromise the success of these students. The extreme students have a difficult time managing their relationships and the pitfalls of their academic journey. Thus, the role of the teacher is to help them define the difference between their emotional reactions and the situations that they are confronted with. The teacher must help them put the situations they are faced with in perspective. Their quest-for-novelty trait can be harnessed in a way that will bring them stimulation because despite their fears and insecurities, they are always open and willing to consider things in a different light.

> Always remember three things with a student that has an extreme profile :
> - Novel stimulations work very well with him because he is receptive to anything that can stimulate and surprise him;
> - Since he fears punishment and the consequences of what he does, he is sensitive to sanctions, mistakes, and risks;
> - Because he does not seek the approval of others and does not care about establishing contacts with others, he is cold and distant, and does not care much about rewards and the attention that can be given to him.

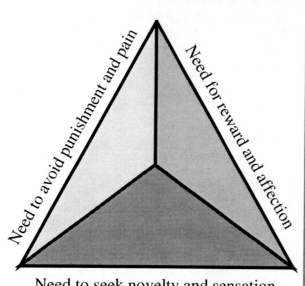

The clever personality is characterized by a strong need to seek novelty, a strong need to avoid punishment and pain, and a strong need for reward and affection.

The clever student has a personality profile that shows a hidden aggressiveness underneath kind manners. Because he has a strong need for reward and affection, he often seeks the approval of others, support, and reinforcement for what he did or said. But his strong need to avoid punishment and pain makes him very careful in his relationships and he almost never dares to assert himself openly. For instance, since he seeks to be liked and appreciated by others on one hand, and does not want to be rejected on the other hand, then this will result in his refusal to venture into the unknown when it comes to establishing relationships with others. Yet, his strong need to seek novelty can make him easily frustrated when he does not achieve what he wants. Indeed, he can become frustrated and aggressive in his relationships with others but will not let these emotions transpire for fear of being rejected or punished if he does so openly. He hides his aggressiveness by harboring ill feelings, by sulking, and above all, by subversively committing actions toward the subject of his ill feelings. In other words, when present his behavior is kind and sweet. But when not present, his behavior is deviant and manipulative.

Let us say, for example, the clever student who works in a group with other students. He does not tolerate others telling him what to do because he does not like to be bossed around. Nor does he like to be criticized or told remarks about his work or involvement within the team. He does everything to show others that he is involved and that he does a good job only to have their approval. But if someone in the team criticizes him openly, saying that he does not work hard enough, is always late, and never progresses in the assignments that he committed to do, then he will not directly and openly show his vexation. He may sulk or withdraw in complete silence but without the knowledge of team-mates, he may complain to the teacher, create turmoil in the team leading to disagreements between students by purposely omitting to write someone's name on a paper, et cetera. When you are alone with him though, he will never express his discomfort, his feelings, or his disagreement. Instead he will use indirect means to reach his goal.

The clever student is not easy to detect at first glance because he always presents himself as positive and kind. The teacher can only notice him through indirect observation and, with time, he will discover that the student always talks behind other students' backs. He is also always on the defensive even though the teacher did not accuse him of any wrongdoing. The teacher may also notice that this type of student does not react well with authority and he will never manifest it directly.

So when dealing with a student that has this type of behavior, the teacher must consider each criticism toward others, each sulk, and each sullen mood as a coded message that the student tries to send. He must question this message by asking the student what is wrong and by inviting him to clearly express himself in order to avoid his bad habit of sending messages that are ambiguous. For instance, if the student criticizes another student, the teacher must tell him that he would like to discuss it in the presence of that other student. If he sulks or gives the teacher an ambiguous message, he must ask him to be clearer. But the teacher must be careful not to criticize him like parents do with their children or patronize him or make reference to good or bad morals. The teacher must simply and tactfully describe what worries him about the student's behavior or what appears to be wrong.

Finally, the teacher must be careful not to be misled in an escalation of reprisals, retributions, or retorts. He must go back to the number one secret in emotional intelligence; encourage the student to clearly express what he is feeling.

> Always remember three things with a student that has a clever profile :
> - Novel stimulations work very well with him because he is receptive to anything that can stimulate and surprise him;
> - Since he fears punishment and the consequences of what he does, he is sensitive to sanctions, mistakes, and risks;
> - Because he seeks the approval of others he does care about rewards and the attention that can be given to him.

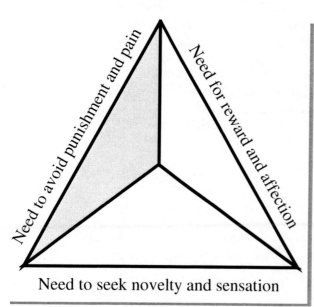

Need to avoid punishment and pain

Need for reward and affection

Need to seek novelty and sensation

The meticulous personality is characterized by a faint need to seek novelty, a strong need to avoid punishment and pain, and a faint need for reward and affection.

With a faint need to seek novelty coupled with a faint need for reward and affection, the meticulous student is a very reserved, shy, and introverted individual. Moreover, his strong need to avoid punishment and pain says that he always wants to do things well. Perhaps this is where his obsession originates. Thus, components such as doubt, structure, quest for perfection, and fear of not doing things right are emotions that invigorate the meticulous student.

This student is relatively easy to detect because he is discreet and not very communicative. He is always well organized, does very beautiful and nicely presented assignments, perhaps spending too much time on the appearance. His work is excessive but conservative, taking no risks. For example, the teacher asks his students to answer one or two questions during the week. While the majority of students return their one-page hand-written homework, the meticulous student returns a typewritten homework often complete with covering page and an impeccable presentation. It is obvious that he spends a great deal of time and energy in his preparation. As a matter of fact, he is always the last one to finish an exam because he spends more time reviewing the questions.

With this profile, it is easy to understand why he does not tolerate failures. For instance, in his assignment, he did a very good job, got a very good score but because the teacher added some comments in the margin, he feels dejected. And this detail is enough to make him forget about the good score that he received and focus on the comments instead.

This behavior will completely deplete his energy. This is why the meticulous is often exhausted and even sick.

The insecurity and the need to be perfect are components that reside in him permanently. When he has a decision to make he is slow and indecisive because he is afraid to make a mistake. What is extremely important for him is to understand what he is being asked and because he does not talk often and is reserved, helping him is not an easy task. However, if the teacher manages to be alone with him in a non-threatening environment it will be easier to help this student and make him aware of the importance to take risks. This can happen by highlighting the quality of his work and by encouraging him to emerge from his withdrawn state so as to stimulate his confidence and creativity.

Chapter 6

Always remember three things with a student that has a meticulous profile :
- Since he does not seek novelty very much, he is very uncomfortable with change;
- Since he fears punishment and the consequences of what he does, he is sensitive to sanctions, mistakes, and risks;
- Because he does not seek the approval of others and does not care about establishing contacts with others, he is cold and distant, and does not care much about rewards and the attention that can be given to him.

The affective personality is characterized by a faint need to seek novelty, a faint need to avoid punishment and pain, and a strong need for reward and affection.

Theoretically, a faint need to seek novelty translates to having little curiosity and enthusiasm as well as a reserved and thoughtful attitude. However, coupling a faint need to avoid punishment and pain with a strong need for reward and affection make the affective student an open, extroverted, warm, sensitive, and highly relational person. It is easy for him to establish relationships but does not necessarily seek novelty and change. As opposed to the theatrical, he preferably seeks stable and long-term relationships.

The faint need to avoid punishment and pain makes the affective an optimistic and relatively relaxed and calm individual. However, his lack of concern can backfire and affect him as well as his relationships.

Since his passion lies in the relational, everything revolves around it even in school. His priorities are his relationships; friends, love, family, and teacher. When his relationships are going well, he is very efficient. However, if there is conflict in his relationships such as an agitated and confusing love relationship, or tension with a close friend then his academic performance will be directly affected. This is why this profile is also labelled as "up and down". In other words, his emotional ties directly affect his mood swings. If all goes well in his relationships, he is happy. And if the relationships are wobbly, then he feels the same. Likewise, if his relationships are bright and pleasant, he is bright and pleasant. And if the relationships are gloomy, then he feels the same. This means that his mood is on the same wavelength as his emotional life.

Two notions are important with regards to the affective type. Firstly, the teacher must have a good rapport with this type of student. This is relatively easy to do

Personality profiles

as this student generally seeks to establish a rapport with the teacher quickly. In other words, he will go to the teacher whether the teacher invites him to come to him or not. Therefore, to help him means to have a liking for him. The teacher must make him feel worthwhile in his eyes and the student will feel good and become more confident.

The other notion is for the teacher to help him strengthen his affective side and learn how to function well in life whatever the state of his relationships is. This type of student must learn to live with his "up and down" demeanor no matter what situation he faces. In short, this student must learn how to distance himself "emotionally" from his relationships. The teacher can help him to refocus his energy where it is needed because his academic grades depend on it directly.

Always remember three things with a student that has an affective profile :
- Since he seeks friendly contacts and the approval of others, he cares a lot about rewards and the attention that can be given to him;
- Since he does not seek novelty very much, he is very uncomfortable with change;
- Since he does not fear punishment and the consequences of what he does, he is insensitive to sanctions and not very shy.

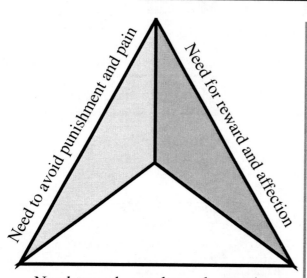

Need to seek novelty and sensation

The docile personality is characterized by a strong need to avoid punishment and pain, a strong need for reward and affection (emotional dependency), and a faint need to seek novelty.

If the mood of the affective personality student is driven by his relationships, we can easily say that the docile personality student (passive and dependent) systematically allows his life to be guided by external events. He is profoundly insecure in his daily activities as much as in his relationships and is very indecisive. He has a tendency to let situations and his friends decide for him, and he does not take any risks whether in his activities or his relationships. He is very slow to react and to commit because he never knows what to do or to decide. His life is filled with the fear of being abandoned. Often times he is inhabited by a feeling of powerlessness and incompetence. He passively subjects himself to the wishes of others and finds it difficult to deal with the demands of daily life. A lack of energy can manifest itself intellectually or emotionally.

Whether at school or at work, the docile student rarely takes the initiative. He does everything that he is being asked to do and nothing more because he as a strong need for reward and affection. Moreover, because of his strong need to avoid punishment and pain, he is fearful of making mistakes or not doing things the right way. This leads him to be less vigilant in his assignments, tasks, and activities. He is a follower and rarely initiates things and is easily influenced in his opinions because he does not want to disappoint others or be rejected.

In addition, he is extremely generous and would give everything if he was asked to do so.

Relationships with a docile student are not simple because no matter what the teacher tells him, he agrees. He offers no resistance which can hinder the teacher's ability to monitor his progress through feedback. He says yes, but acts very little. He does not want to be wrong (fear of punishment) and he wants to please (affective need). He also is very comfortable with familiar things and routine (faint need to seek novelty). So he repeats the same things over and over.

> Always remember three things with a student that has a docile profile :
> - Since he does not seek novelty very much, he is very uncomfortable with change;
> - Since he fears punishment and the consequences of what he does, he is sensitive to sanctions, mistakes, and risks;
> - Since he seeks friendly contacts and the approval of others, he cares a lot about rewards and the attention that can be given to him.

The Hermit is characterized by a faint need to seek novelty, a faint need to avoid punishment and pain, and a faint need for reward and affection.

Let us say on the outset that this profile is very rare and at a high risk of leading to a drop out. The combination of a faint need in all three dimensions of personality places us in front of an individual who lives a life of withdrawal from social and affective contacts. Thus, it allows him to put the emphasis on his internal world, solitude, and introspection.

The hermit personality does not seek nor appreciates establishing close relationships even with members of his family. Instead he almost always chooses solo activities. He has little to no interest in sexual relationships with other people and seldom feels pleasure in activities. This is why it is very difficult to keep him in an academic

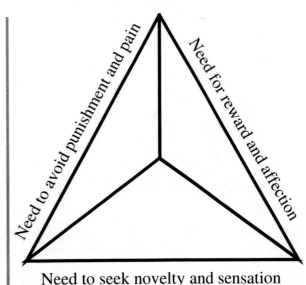

environment. He does not have close friends or people he can confide in. He is indifferent to praises and can seem very cold and detached.

It is as if nothing affected him. To use a popular expression : "A bomb could fall next to him, and he would not even twitch."

Therefore, trying to make this type of student aware of the negative consequences of his actions is futile. Equally futile is to make him look at the positive side of things as they mean nothing to him and he feels no connection whatsoever to these things. Novelty does not interest him either. However, since he has a faint need to seek novelty and to avoid punishment and pain, it is possible that he may appreciate routine activities. It is even possible that he may also practice rituals in his personal life. The teacher must find out what his interests are so that he can establish how school can better serve him. Indeed, it is important to address him this way because it is most likely the only way to find a solution that will positively touch his personality.

> Always remember three things with a student that has a hermit profile :
> - Since he does not seek novelty very much, he is very uncomfortable with change;
> - Since he does not fear punishment and the consequences of what he does, he is insensitive to sanctions and threats;
> - Because he does not seek the approval of others and does not care about establishing contacts with others, he is cold and distant, and does not care much about rewards and the attention that can be given to him.

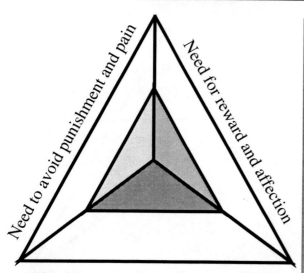

Need to avoid punishment and pain

Need for reward and affection

Need to seek novelty and sensation

The flexible is characterized by an average need for novelty, an average need to avoid punishment and pain, and an average need for reward and affection. As the name indicates, the student with a flexible personality as a relatively easy profile because since he has an average need in all three dimensions of personality, any way you approach him will work. Without being excessive in any of these traits, this type of student is flexible and open to different approaches.

Stability, constancy, and moderation are his main qualities. He is not hyperactive yet, he is not cold or distant either. He enjoys novelty but not in excess. He responds normally to punishment and has a moderate threshold for pain. He also appreciates rewards and signs of affective attention given to him but is not dependent of them. In short, every

Chapter 6

teacher would want to have students who fit this profile in their classroom. However, human nature is such that all colors exist in this diverse world and this is what makes it beautiful.

How to recognize each of the personality profiles

By referring to table 6.5 below, you will identify signs of the three components of personality necessary to recognize your students' profiles.

Table 6.5
Signs of each of the components of personality

Components of the need to seek novelty	
People with a faint need to seek novelty have a tendency to :	People with a strong need to seek novelty have a tendency to :
Seek routine and familiar situations. Want to be persuaded of the advantages before adopting a new approach.	Explore new and unfamiliar situations. Be swift to commit to new ideas and approaches. Get bored with routine.
Analyze details before making a decision. Able to think and concentrate for a long period of time.	Be impulsive. Make decisions based on their intuition and emotions, without thinking.
Be reserved, have self-control and self-discipline. Not waste their time, money, and their energy.	Be extravagant and try to impress others. Not be very thrifty. Have a hard time to manage their time, money, and energy.
Be tidy, organized, and methodical. Follow the rules. Be patient and tolerate frustration.	Be messy, not very methodical, unorganized. Reject the rules. Avoid uncomfortable and frustrating situations.
Components of the need to avoid punishment and pain	
People with a faint need to avoid punishment and pain have a tendency to :	People with a strong need to avoid punishment and pain have a tendency to :
Be optimistic and not worry when facing difficulties. Be unconcerned and nonchalant. Not be afraid of taking risks.	Worry and anticipate misfortune and failure in everything they do. Struggle to recover from failure and humiliation.
Be confident, calm, and secure in almost any situation. Take risks. Easily adapt to change and unforeseen situations.	Not tolerate uncertainty and be apprehensive of the unknown. Not take a lot of risks. Struggle to adapt to change.

Personality profiles

Be bold and open. Be direct. Not be shy or uncomfortable with novelty.	Be shy and lack self-confidence in social situations. Avoid unfamiliar contacts. Need tangible signs of acceptance before establishing contact with someone.
Be energetic and invigorated. Have endurance when making an effort and recover quickly.	Be asthenic and have less energy than the average person. Need rest to recuperate. Recover slowly from fatigue, sickness, or stress.

Components of the need for reward and affection

People with a faint need for reward and affection have a tendency to :	People with a strong need for reward and affection have a tendency to :
Be cold and detached. Lack empathy and compassion. Be less inclined to become sentimental and romantic.	Easily show their emotions. Live intensely the emotions of others. Be sentimental, compassionate, and receptive to the emotions of others.
Be lonely and reserved when it comes to their privacy. Be less interested in social relationships.	Seek intimacy. Openly speak about how they feel and their private life. Seek long-term relationships. Be sensitive to rejection.
Be independent, self-sufficient, and insensitive to social pressure, criticism, or rejection. Not seek the approval of others and not seek to please others. Rarely submit to others' desires	Be dependent on the opinions of others. Seek the approval of others and seek to please others. Be afraid of rejection and being abandoned. Be sensitive to signs of social rejection or disapproval. Change their mind just to please.
Be lethargic, inactive, and unstable. Be unreliable. Not work harder even if a reward is anticipated. Not be uplifted by a salary, good grade, or good score. Not tolerate frustration. Give up when frustrated. Not try to surpass themselves.	Be hard workers, persistent, and persevering. Be generous and always there to help. Double up their effort when a reward is anticipated. Be perfectionists and constantly seek to improve themselves.

Stimulating students according to their personality profile

In the beginning of this chapter we mentioned that the way we feel and react to stimuli from our environment will differ considerably from one individual to another. With this in mind, we were able to assess that using the three innate components of personality, as discovered by Robert Cloninger, we do not react the same way and to the same things. For instance, some react more strongly to novelty while others are destabilized by it. Some have a very high threshold for punishment and pain while others are very sensitive to it. Finally, some are more inclined to reward and social reinforcements while others find no appeal in it.

Table 6.6 illustrates each of the nine personality profiles, their emotional characteristics and their dominant needs. The table also gives suggestions to the teacher for each of them.

Table 6.6
The nine personality profiles and their characteristics

Personality Profiles	Emotional Characteristics	Dominant Needs	Suggestions for the teacher
Bold	Negative - Aggressiveness - Lack of concern - Insensitive - Lack of empathy Positive - Calm - Courageous	- To be stimulated - To seek novelty - To be different	Stimulate him with novelty Use humor and metaphors Encourage him to go in unorthodox directions in his assignments Avoid irritating him Encourage him to express his difference and invite him to do the same for others Give him challenges
	Negative - Sadness - Anger - Unstability - Inconstancy Positive - Curiosity	- To feel appreciated - To feel recognized - To feel admired - To feel	Avoid threatening him with punishment Give him your attention only if he deserves it

Theatrical (triangle diagram: Need to avoid punishment and pain / Need for reward and affection / Need to seek novelty and sensation)	- Joyful - Courageous	useful - To seek novelty - To shine	Give him an opportunity to bring out his best Propose new experiences to him Call for his tremendous creativity
Extreme (triangle diagram: Need to avoid punishment and pain / Need for reward and affection / Need to seek novelty and sensation)	Negative - Fear - Fiery - Impulsive - Unstable - Anxious - Insecure Positive - Open - Passionate	- To feel reassured - To feel appraised - To seek novelty	Avoid putting pressure on him Help him differentiate the facts, his interpretations, and his emotions Help him to put everything in perspective Stimulate him with new things while making him feel that it's okay
Clever (triangle diagram: Need to avoid punishment and pain / Need for reward and affection / Need to seek novelty and sensation)	Negative - Fear - Sadness - Aggressiveness - Insecurity Positive - Joyful - Kindness	- To be approved of - To be right - To be loved - To control	Question him about his behaviors and his reactions Invite him to express himself clearly Start the discussion when alone with him Avoid criticizing and patronizing him like parents do with their children

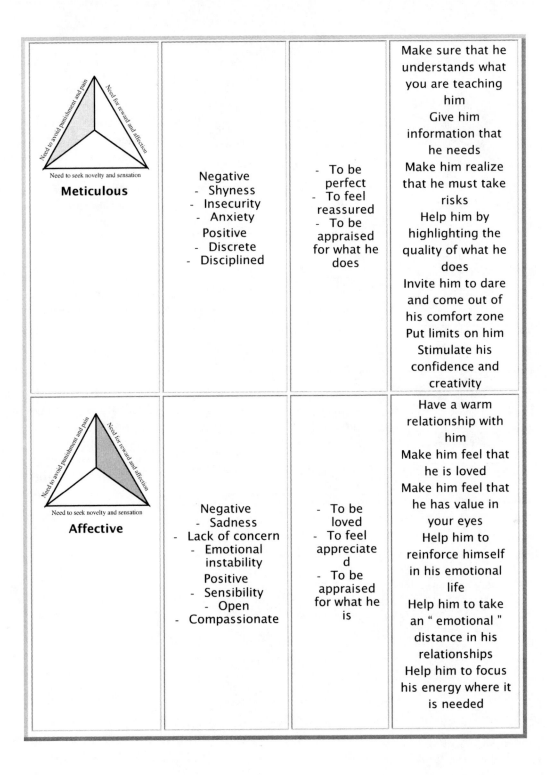

Meticulous	Negative - Shyness - Insecurity - Anxiety Positive - Discrete - Disciplined	- To be perfect - To feel reassured - To be appraised for what he does	Make sure that he understands what you are teaching him Give him information that he needs Make him realize that he must take risks Help him by highlighting the quality of what he does Invite him to dare and come out of his comfort zone Put limits on him Stimulate his confidence and creativity
Affective	Negative - Sadness - Lack of concern - Emotional instability Positive - Sensibility - Open - Compassionate	- To be loved - To feel appreciated - To be appraised for what he is	Have a warm relationship with him Make him feel that he is loved Make him feel that he has value in your eyes Help him to reinforce himself in his emotional life Help him to take an " emotional " distance in his relationships Help him to focus his energy where it is needed

Personality profiles

 Docile	Negative - Sadness - Fear - Insecurity - Anxiety Positive - Sensibility - Generosity - Kindness	- To be loved - To be reassured - To feel appreciated	Address him with warmth Clearly express your expectations of him Help him to assert himself and express his point of view Help him to take risks Help him to take the initiative
 Hermit	Negative - Indifference Positive - Stability	- To feel regular	Ask him what his interests are in order to see how school can help him fulfill them Address him through his interests Propose routine activities to him
 Flexible	Negative - Sometimes difficulty to understand Positive - Flexibility	- Variety - A good dose of love, reward, novelty, and reassurance	Trust him Vary and experiment different angles from which to address him (novelty, punishment, and reinforcement)

Chapter 6

Conclusion

A lthough the action of reading a book involves the 'cognitive' brain, throughout this book, we have insisted on the fact that the true learning process did not involve the 'cognitive' but rather the 'emotional' brain. We hope that reading this book has awakened within you the desire to further "touch" the individuals you are imparting knowledge to. Equally sincere is our hope that you not only understood this book but also felt what it tried to impart so that you can apply its value to your daily reality as a teacher and educator.

We are also aware that despite the cognition exercises and the teaching tools provided in this book, the depth with which emotional pedagogy can be integrated reaches far beyond. This is why we created the EPI (Emotional Pedagogy Institute), so as to offer seminars and trainings designed to deepen the theoretical aspects of this book. In addition to delivering Emotional Pedagogy, our trainings represent the real-time application of this notion. They can also be accredited for those who wish to incorporate emotional pedagogy in their environment.

We firmly believe in this approach and hope that it will soon spread very fast. Human beings are sensitive; they need to feel in order to learn.

To contact us :

Emotional Pedagogy Institute (EPI)
PO BOX 47054
CP Place LaSalle
LaSalle, Qc.
Canada
H8P 3V9
Phone: 514-365-8290
Fax: 514-365-7837
Email: epi@emotionalpedagogy.com

www.emotionalpedagogy.com

References

Aftanas L.I. Golocheikine S.A. (2001). Human anterior and frontal midline theta and lower alpha reflect emotionally positive state and internalized attention : high-resolution EEG investigation of meditation. *Neuroscience letters*, vol. 310(1), p. 57-60.

al'Absi M, Hugdahl K, Lovallo W.R. (2002). Adrenocortical stress responses and altered working memory performance. *Psychophysiology*, vol. 39(1), p. 95-99.

Assor A, Kaplan H, Roth G. (2002). Choice is good, but relevance is excellent : autonomy-enhancing and suppressing teacher behaviors predicting students' engagement in schoolwork. *The British journal of educational psychology*, vol. 72(Pt 2), p. 261-278.

Baving L, Laucht M, Schmidt MH. (2002). Frontal brain activation in anxious school children. *Journal of child psychology and psychiatry, and allied disciplines*, 43(2), p. 265-74.

Benson E (2002) : The synaptic self without synaptic plasticity, learning--and the self--would be impossible, Monitor on psychology, *American Psychological Association*, Volume 33, No. 10 November 2002.

Benson, H. (1975). *The relaxation response*, New-York, Morrow.

Berry D.S., Pennebaker J.W. (1993). Nonverbal and verbal emotional expression and health. *Psychotherapy and psychosomatics*, vol. 59(1), p. 11-19.

Bischof-Kohler D. (1994). Self object and interpersonal emotions. Identification of own mirror image, empathy and prosocial behavior in the 2nd year of life. Z *Psychol Z Angew Psychol*, vol. 202(4), p. 349-377.

Bloch, S. (1989). [Emotion felt, emotion recreated], [Article in French] *Science & Vie*, no. 168, p. 68-75.

Boone R.T., Cunningham J.G., (1998). Children's decoding of emotion in expressive body movement : the development of cue attunement. *Developmental psychology*, vol.34(5), p.1007-1016.

Boyatzis, R. (2002). *Core Competencies in Coaching Others to Overcome Dysfunctional Behavior.*, in : www.eiconsortium.org.

Bremner J.D. (2002). Neuroimaging of childhood trauma. Seminars in Clinical *Neuropsychiatry*, vol. 7(2) :104-12.

Bremner J.D. (2002). Neuroimaging studies in post-traumatic stress disorder. *Current psychiatry reports*, vol. 4(4), p. 254-63.

Breur, H. (2003). [Neurons of sympathy] [Article in French] *Cerveau & psycho*, no. 1, p.40-41.

Statistical Report of Education, [*School abandons and drop outs*] [Article in French] les concepts. No. 25, Mars 2003, Quebec Ministry of Education, in : www.meq.gouv.qc.ca

Carr, L., Iacoboni, M., Dubeau, M.-C., Mazziotta, J.C., and Lenzi G.L., "Neural mechanisms of empathy in humans : A relay from neural systems for imitation to limbic areas", *Proc. Natl. Acad. Sci. USA*, 100 :5497-5502 (2003).

Chabot, D. (1996). [*Emotions and adaptation*] [Book in French] CCFG and Quebec Ministry of Education.

Chabot, D. (1998). [*Foster your emotional intelligence*] [Book in French] Montreal : Quebecor.

Chabot, D. (2000). [*Magical pleasure, pleasurology*] [Book in French] Montreal : Quebecor. p. 110

Choi, C. (2003). *Brain feels empathy by imitation*, in : www.upi.com/view.cfm?StoryID=2003 0405-081743-6763r

Cloninger C.R., Svrakic D.M., Przybeck T.R. (1993). A psychobiological model of temperament and character. *Archives of general psychiatry*, vol 50(12), p. 975-990.

Coffman, Stephan L. (1981). Empathy as a Relevant Instructor Variable in the *Experiential Classroom. Group and Organization Studies*, vol. 6, p. 114-120.

Colt, E.W., Wardlaw S.L.and Frantz A.G. (1981). The effect of running on plasma ß-endorphin, *Life Sciences*, no 28, p. 1637-1640.

Comunian A.L. (1993). Anxiety, cognitive interference, and school performance of Italian children. *Psychol Rep*, vol. 73(3 Pt 1), p. 747-54.

Cormier N. and Julien, D. (1996). [Relationship between marital adjustments and subjective and objective measures of conjugal support] [Article in French] *Canadian Journal of Behavioral Science*, Volume 28, no 4.

Cyrulnik, B. 1999). [*A wonderful misfortune*] [Book in French] Paris, Odile Jacob publisher.

Damasio, A. (1994). *Descartes' Error, Emotion, Reason and the Human Brain.* New York : Putnam Books.

Damasio, A. (1999). *The feeling of What Happens. Body and Emotion in the Making of Consciousness.* New York : Harcourt Brace & Compagny.

Davidson R.J. (2000). Affective style, psychopathology, and resilience : brain mechanisms and plasticity. *The American psychologist*, vol. 55(11) : 1196-214.

Davidson R.J., Lewis D.A., Alloy LB, Amaral D.G., Bush G., Cohen J.D., Drevets W.C., Farah M.J., Kagan J., McClelland J.L., Nolen-Hoeksema S., Peterson B.S. (2002) : Neural and behavioral substrates of mood and mood regulation, *Biological psychiatry*, 52(6) :478-502.

Davidson, R. (1987) : [Well divided humors] [Article in French] *Science & Vie (hors-series)*, 168 : 50-57.

Davidson, R. J., Kabat-Zinn, J., Schumacher, J., Rosenkrantz, M., Muller, D., Santorelli, S. F. et al. (2003). Alterations in brain and immune function produced by mindfulness meditation. *Psychosomatic Medicine*,65, 564-570.

Davidson, R.J. (1998) : Affective style and Affective disorders : Perspectives from Affective Neuroscience. *Cognition and Emotion* : 12(3), 307-330.

Davidson, R.J. (2001). Toward a Biology of Personality and Emotion, *Annals of the New York Academy of Sciences*, 935, 191-207.

Davidson, R. J. (2002). Toward a biology of positive affect and compassion. In R.J.Davidson & A. Harrington (Eds.), *Vision of Compassion : Western Scientists and Tibetan Buddhists Examine Human Nature.* (pp. 107-130). New York : Oxford University Press.

Delmonte, M.M. (1985). Biochemical indices associated with meditation practice : a litterature review, *Biobehavioral Reviews*, no 9, p. 557-561.

Dolan, R.J. (2002). Emotion, cognition, and behavior. *Science*, 298, p. 1191-1194.

Dughiero G, Schifano F, Forza G. (2001). Personality dimensions and psychopathological profiles of Ecstasy users. *Human psychopharmacology*, vol. 16(8), p. 635-639.

Ekman, Paul (2003). *Emotions revealed : recognizing faces and feelings to improve communicatioin and emotional life*, New York : Times Books, Henry Holt and Company.

Ekman, P. & Davidson, R.J. (1993). Volontary smiling changes regional brain activity. *Psychological Science*, vol. 4, p. 342-345.

Ekman, P. (1996). Why Don't We Catch Liars? *Social Research*, Vol. 63 (3), p. 801-817.

Ekman, P., Levenson R. W. and Friesen W.V. (1983). Autonomic nervous system activity distinguishes among emotions. *Science*, no 221, p. 1208-1210.

Ekman, Paul (1982). *Emotion in the human face, Second Edition.* Cambridge University Press.

Etcoff N.L., Ekman P., Magee J.J., Frank M.G. (2000). Lie detection and language comprehension. *Nature*, vol. 405 (6783), p.139.

Eustachem F. (2000). [Still images] [Article in French] *Science & Vie*, no 212, p. 66-73.

Field, T., & Walden, T. (1982). Production and discrimination of facial expressions by preschool children. *Child Development*, 53, p. 1299-1311.

Fox N.A., Rubin K.H., Calkins S.D., Marshall T.R., Coplan R.J., Porges S.W., Long J.M., Stewart S. (1995). Frontal activation asymmetry and social competence at four years of age. *Child Development*, vol. 66(6), p. 1770-1784.

Gardner, H. (1983), *Frames of minds : the theory of multiple intelligences.* New York : Basic books.

Goleman, D. (1995). *Emotional Intelligence : Why it can matter more than IQ.* New York : Bantam.

Goleman, D., Boyatzis, R. & McKee, A. (2002). *Primal Leadership : Realizing the Power of Emotional Intelligence.* Boston : Harvard Business Press.

Emotional Pedagogy

Gosselin, P. (1995). [The development of the recognition of emotional facial expressions in children] [Article in French] *La revue canadienne des sciences du comportement*, vol. 27, no. 2.

Gottman, J. M. et Silver, N. (2000). *The Seven Principles for Making Marriage Work : A Practical Guide from the Country's Foremost Relationship Expert*. Three Rivers Press.

Grover P.L. & Smith D.U. (1981). Academic anxiety, locus of control, and achievement in medical school. *Journal of medical Education*, vol 56 (9 Pt 1), p. 727-36.

Hansenne M., Ansseau M. (1999). Harm avoidance and serotonin. *Biological Psychology*, vol. 51(1), p. 77-81.

Hansenne M., Reggers J., Pinto E., Kjiri K., Ajamier A., Ansseau M. (1999). Temperament and character inventory (TCI) and depression. *Journal of psychiatric research*, vol. 33(1), p. 31-36.

Harmel Kristin (2000), *Gifted students are more imaginative and emotional, UF study shows*, in www.sciencedaily.com/releases/2000/07/000710120608.htm.

Hopko D.R., Ashcraft M.H., Gute J., Ruggiero K.J., Lewis C. (1998). Mathematics anxiety and working memory : support for the existence of a deficient inhibition mechanism. *Journal of Anxiety Disorder*, vol. 12(4), p. 343-355.

Howden, J. and Kopiec, M. (2000). [*Adding to skills : teaching, cooperating and learning after highschool*] [Book in French] Montreal : Chenelière/McGraw-Hill.

Huffman, K., M. Vernoy and J. Vernoy (2000). *Psychology in Action*. Fifth Edition, John Wiley and Sons Inc.

Hughes C., White A., Sharpen J., Dunn J. (2000). Antisocial, angry, and unsympathetic : "hard-to-manage" preschoolers' peer problems and possible cognitive influences. *Journal of child psychology and psychiatry, and allied disciplines*, vol. 41(2) :169-79.

Jaffard, R. (2000). [The labyrinths of animal memory] [Article in French] *Science & Vie*, no 212, p. 44-51.

Janelle C.M. (2002). Anxiety, arousal and visual attention : a mechanistic account of performance variability. *Journal of sports sciences*, vol. 20(3), p. 237-51.

Janowiak J.J., Hackman R. (1994). Meditation and college students' self-actualization and rated stress. *Psychol Rep*, vol. 75(2), p.1007-1010.

Jevning, R., Wilson, A.F. and Smith W.R. (1978). The transcendental meditation technique, adrenocortical activity and implications for stress, *Experientia,* no 34, p. 618-619.

John P.K., Blackhart G.C., Woodward, K.M. Williams S.R. and Schwartz G.E.R. (2000) Anterior electroencephalographic asymmetry changes in elderly women in response to a pleasant and an unpleasant odor, *Biological Psychology*, vol. 52(3), p. 241-250.

Jones N.A., Field T. (1999). Massage and music therapies attenuate frontal EEG asymmetry in depressed adolescents. *Adolescence* vol. 34(135), p. 529-534.

Kalant H. (2001). The pharmacology and toxicology of "ecstasy" (MDMA) and related drugs. *Canadian Medical Association journal*, vol. 165(7), p. 917-928.

Kellogg J.S., Hopko D.R., Ashcraft M.H. (1999). The effects of time pressure on arithmetic performance. *Journal of Anxiety Disorders*, vol. 13(6) p. 591-600.

Kirsh S.J., Olczak P.V. (2002). Violent comic books and judgments of relational aggression. *Violence Vict*, vol. 17(3), p. 373-80.

Kolb, B., & Whishaw, I. Q. (1996). *Keys of human neuropsychology (4th edition)*. San Francisco : W.H. Freeman.

Krause N. (2003). Religious meaning and subjective well-being in late life. *The journals of gerontology. Series B, Psychological sciences and social sciences.* vol. 58(3), p. 160-170.

Labarbera, J.D., Izard, C.E., Vietze, P., & Parisi, S.A. (1976). Four-and six-month-old infants' visual responses to joy, anger, and neutral expressions. *Child Development*, 47, p. 535-538.

Laird, J. D. (1974). Self-attribution of emotions : the effects of expressive behavior on the quality of emotional experience. *Journal of personality and social psychology*, no 29, p. 475-486.

References

Lane R.D. Sechrest L., Reidel R., Weldon V, Kaszniak A, Schwartz G.E. (1996). Impaired verbal and nonverbal emotion recognition in alexithymia. *Psychosomatic Medicine*, vol. 58(6), p. 581.

Larson, C.L., Sutton, S.K., & Davidson, R.J. (1998). Affective style, frontal EEG asymmetry and time course of the emotion-modulated startle. Psychophysiology, vol. 35, S52.

Lazarus, R. S. (1991). *Emotion and adaptation*, New York, Oxford University Press.

LeDoux, J. (2001). [Fear and unconscious memory] [Article in French] *Pour la Science*, dossier no.31, p. 104-109.

Ledoux, J.E. (1994) : Emotion, memory and the brain, *Scientific American* : 270(6) :50-7.

Lenti C, Lenti-Boero D, Giacobbe A. (1999). Decoding of emotional expressions in children and adolescents. *Perceptual and motor skills*, vol. 89(3 Pt 1), p. 808-814.

Leon M.R., Revelle W. (1985). Effects of anxiety on analogical reasoning : a test of three theoretical models. *Journal of personality and social psychology*, vol. 49(5), p. 1302-1315.

Lieberman, J.A., Stuard, M.R. (1999). The BATHE Method : incorporating counseling and psychotherapy into the everyday management of patients. *Journal of Clinical Psychiatry*, Vol. 1 (2), p. 35-39.

Malatesta C.Z., Izard C.E., Culver C., Nicolich M. (1987). Emotion communication skills in young, middle-aged, and older women. *Psychological Aging*, vol. 2(2) :193-203.

Malathi A, Damodaran A. (1999). Stress due to exams in medical students--role of yoga. *Indian Journal of Physiology andl Pharmacology*, vol. 43(2), p. 218-224.

Mayer, J. D. & Salovey, P. (1997). What is emotional intelligence? In P. Salovey & D. Sluyter (Eds). *Emotional Development and Emotional Intelligence : Implications for Educators* (p. 3-31). New York : Basic Books.

McCraty, R. (2002). *The scientific role of the heart in learning and performance*. Institute of HeartMath.

McCraty, R., Tomasino, D., Atkinson, M. Aasen, P., Thurik, S. J..

(2000). Improving Test-Taking Skills and Academic Performance in High School Students Using HeartMath Learning Enhancement Tools. *HeartMath Research Center, Institute of HeartMath*. Publication No. 00-010. Boulder Creek, CA.

McCook, A. (2003). When you hurt, my brain says I hurt, too : study. http ://healthinfo.carolinas.org/HealthNew s/reuters/NewsStory032520031.htm

Mook, D.G. (1987). *Motivation, the organization of action*, New York, W. W. Norton and Co.

Morgan, W.P. and Horstmann D.H. (1976). Anxiety reduction following acute physical activity, *Medicine and Science in Sports*, vol. 8, p. 62.

Newberg A, Alavi A, Baime M, Pourdehnad M, Santanna J, d'Aquili E. (2001). The measurement of regional cerebral blood flow during the complex cognitive task of meditation : a preliminary SPECT study. *Psychiatry Research*, vol. 106(2), p. 113-22.

Nowicki S., Duke M. (1989). A measure of nonverbal social processing ability in children between 6 and 10. *Paper presented at the American Psychological Society Meeting*.

Öhman, A. (2001). [Memory and phobia] [Article in French] Pour la Science, dossier no.31, p. 110-115.

OECD (2002). *Understanding the Brain, toward a new learning science*. Paris : OECD Publications Services.

Pelletier, L. G. and Vallerand, R. J. (1993). [A humanist perspective of motivation : theories of competence and self-determination. R. J. Vallerand and E. E. Thil] [Book in French] *Introduction à la psychologie de la motivation*, Montréal, Études Vivantes, p. 233-281.

Phelps, E. (2000). [When the emotion reinforces memory] [Article in French] *Science & Vie*, no 212, p. 94-98.

Phillips L.H., MacLean R.D., Allen R. (2002). Age and the understanding of emotions : neuropsychological and sociocognitive perspectives. *The journals of gerontology. Series B, Psychological sciences and social sciences* vol. 57(6), p. 526-530.

Reynolds W.J., Scott B. (1999). Empathy : a crucial component of the helping

Emotional Pedagogy

relationship. *Journal of psychiatric and mental health nursing*, vol. 6(5), p. 363-370.

Rogers, C.R. (1961). On becoming a person. Boston : Houghton Mifflin.

Rosenberg, M. B. (1999). *Nonviolent Communication : A Language of Compassion.* PuddleDancer press.

Rudrauf, D. (2003). [To feel in order to learn] [Article in French] *Science & Vie,* no. 222, p. 82-91.

Salovey P. & D. Sluyter. (1997). *Emotional Development and Emotional Intelligence : Implications for Educators,* New York : Basic Books.

Salovey, P. & Mayer, J.D. (1990). Emotional intelligence. *Imagination, Cognition, and Personality,* 9, 185-211.

Savitsky J.C., Czyzewski D. (1978). The reaction of adolescent offenders and nonoffenders to nonverbal emotion displays. *Journal of abnormal child psychology,* vol, 6(1), p. 89-96.

Searching For Meaning In Life May Boost Immune System. In : www.sciencedaily.com/releases/2003/04/030429083520.htm :

Seipp. B. (1991). Anxiety and academic performance : a meta-analysis. *Anxiety research,* vol. 4 (1).

Servan-Schreiber, D. (2004). *The Instinct to Heal : Curing Stress, Anxiety, and Depression Without Drugs and Without Talk Therapy.* St-Martins Press.

Shah A.H., Joshi S.V., Mehrotra P.P., Potdar N, Dhar H.L. (2001). Effect of Saral meditation on intelligence, performance and cardiopulmonary functions. *Indian Journal of Medical Science,* vol. 55(11), p. 604-608.

Shapiro K. L, Lim A. (1989). The impact of anxiety on visual attention to central and peripheral events. *Behavior research and therapy.* Vol. 27(4), p. 345-51.

Shapiro S.L., Schwartz G.E., Bonner G. (1998). Effects of mindfulness-based stress reduction on medical and premedical students. *Journal of behavioral medicine ,* vol. 21(6), p. 581-599.

Shapiro S.L., Shapiro D.E., Schwartz G.E. (2000). Stress management in medical education : a review of the literature. Academic medicine : *journal of the Association of American Medical Colleges,* vol. 75(7), p. 748-759.

Sobotka S.S., Davidson R.J., Senulis J.A. (1992) : Anterior brain electrical asymmetries in response to reward and punishment. *Electroencephalography and clinical neurophysiology.* ;83(4) :236-47.

Solomon, R.L. (1980). The opponent-process theory of acquired motivation : the costs of pleasure and the benefits of pain. American Psychologist, 35, 691-712.

Souccar, T. (2001). [The biology of personality] [Article in French] *Sciences et avenir,* no 652, p. 57-64.

Spearman, C.(1927), *The abilities of man,* London : Macmillan.

Squire, L. and Kandel. E. (2001). [The memory of skills] [Article in French] *Pour la science,* dossier no 31, p. 86-93.

Steptoe A, Butler N. (1996). Sports participation and emotional well-being in adolescents, *Lancet,* vol. 347(9018), p. 1789-1792.

Sternberg, R. (1988). *The triarchic mind : A new theory of human inteligence.* New York : Viking.

Stewart S.M., Lam T.H., Betson C.L., Wong C.M., Wong A.M. (1999). A prospective analysis of stress and academic performance in the first two years of medical school. *Medical education.,* vol. 33(4), p. 243-50.

Strack, F., Martin L.L. and Stepper S. (1988). Inhibiting and facilitating conditions of the human smile : A nonobstructive test of facial feedback hypothesis. *Journal of Personality and Social Psychology,* no 54, p. 768-777.

Strickland, D. (2000). Emotional intelligence : the most potent factor in the success equation. *Journal of Nursing Administration,* vol. 30 (3), p. 112-117.

Tardif, J. (1997). [*For a strategic teaching, the contributions of cognitive psychology*] [Book in French] Montreal : Les editions Logiques.

Terry W.S., Burns J.S. (2001). Anxiety and repression in attention and retention. The *Journal of general psychology,* vol. 128(4), p. 422-32.

Tomarken A.J., Davidson R.J., Wheeler R.E., Doss R.C. (1992). Individual differences in anterior brain asymmetry and key dimensions of emotion. *Journal of personality and social psychology,* vol. 62(4), p. 676-87.

References

Tomarken A.J., Davidson R.J., Henriques J.B. (1990). Resting frontal brain asymmetry predicts affective responses to films. *Journal of personality and social psychology*, vol. 59(4), p. 791-801.

Uma K, Nagendra H.R, Nagarathna R, Vaidehi S, Seethalakshmi R. (1989). The integrated approach of yoga : a therapeutic tool for mentally retarded children : a one-year controlled study. *Journal of Mental Deficit Research*, vol. 33 (Pt 5), p. 415-21.

Vallerand, R. J. (1993). [Intrinsic and extrinsic motivation in a natural context : implications for the areas of education, work, interpersonal relationships and leisures] [Book in French] R. J. Vallerand and E. E. Thil, *Introduction à la psychologie de la motivation*, Montréal, Études Vivantes, p. 533-581.

Watson, J. B., and R. Rayner. (1920) Conditioned emotional reactions. *Journal of experimental Psychology*, no. 3, p. 1-14.

Wingerson D., Sullivan M., Dager S., Flick S., Dunner D., Roy-Byrne P. (1993). Personality traits and early discontinuation from clinical trials in anxious patients. *Journal of clinical psychopharmacology*, vol. 13(3), p. 194-197.

Index

ISBN 1-41204219-4

9 781412 042192